Religion and Cult

Religion and Cult

*The Old Testament
and the Phenomenology of Religion*

SIGMUND MOWINCKEL

Translated by John F. X. Sheehan

Edited by K. C. Hanson

CASCADE *Books* · Eugene, Oregon

RELIGION AND CULT
The Old Testament and the Phenomenology of Religion

Copyright © 2012 and 1950 the Estate of Sigmund Mowinckel. Translation © 1981 Marquette University Press. All rights reserved. Except for brief quotations in critical publications or reviews, no part of this book may be reproduced in any manner without prior written permission from the publisher. Write: Permissions, Wipf and Stock Publishers, 199 W. 8th Ave., Suite 3, Eugene, OR 97401.

Cascade Books
An Imprint of Wipf and Stock Publishers
199 W. 8th Ave., Suite 3
Eugene, OR 97401

www.wipfandstock.com

isbn 13: 978-1-62032-043-3

Cataloging-in-Publication data:

Mowinckel, Sigmund, 1884–1965.

    Religion and cult : the Old Testament and the phenomenology of religion / Sigmund Mowinckel ; translated by John F. X. Sheehan ; edited by K. C. Hanson.

    xii + 200 p. ; 23 cm. Including bibliographical references and indexes.

    Translation of Religion og kultus, 1971.

    ISBN 13: 978-1-62032-043-3

    1. Religion—Philosophy. 2. Worship in the Bible. 3. Public worship in the Bible. I. Sheehan, John F. X. II. Hanson, K. C. (Kenneth Charles). III. Title.

BL550 M61 2012

Manufactured in the U.S.A.

Scripture quotations are from the New Revised Standard Version of the Bible, copyright © 1989 by the Division of Christian Education of the National Council of Churches of Christ in the USA and used by permission.

Contents

Translator's Note · vii

Editor's Foreword · ix

Abbreviations · xiii

1. Religion and Its Manifestations · 1
2. The Meaning of Cult · 5
3. The Magical Perception of Reality · 8
4. Magic and Religion · 24
5. Holiness and the Holy One · 29
6. Fellowship: God and Congregation · 45
7. Established Orders · 52
8. The Goals of Worship · 59
9. The Cycle: The Renewal of Life · 72
10. The Creating Drama · 77
11. Prophecy and Mysticism · 87
12. The Cultic Myth: Belief and Confession · 92
13. Cultic Actions · 98
14. Cultic Words · 111
15. Prayers and Psalms · 121

Contents

16 Worship and Morality · 130

17 Impurity, Sin, and Purification · 135

18 The Problem of the Origin of Religion · 147

19 Overview · 157

The Works of Sigmund Mowinckel in English · 159

Recommended Readings · 163

Bibliography · 175

Index of Ancient Documents · 183

Index of Subjects · 191

Index of Authors · 197

Translator's Note

Even an "experimental edition" of a book like this cannot be produced without assistance. It is a pleasure to thank the Marquette Jesuits for their most recent of many kindnesses. It is also a pleasure to thank the Vincentians of Princeton, New Jersey, and the St. Josefsøstrene of Oslo, Norway. Without their gracious hospitality, the ongoing education of a certain *clericus vagans* would have been much harder to come by.

Feast of St. Sylvester
December 31, 1980
J. Sheehan, SJ

Editor's Foreword

This volume has a long and complicated history. Sigmund Mowinckel wrote the original manuscript in Norwegian and published it in 1950 and reprinted in 1971 (*Religion og Kultus*), based on lectures he had given to theology students at the University of Oslo. It was translated into German by Albrecht Schauer with slightly expanded notes in 1953 (*Religion und Kultus*). Father John F. X. Sheehan, SJ, translated the Norwegian edition, completing it at the end of 1980, and the typescript was distributed in a limited way by Marquette University in 1981. In this edition, I have thoroughly edited Fr. Sheehan's translation.

∼

Sigmund Mowinckel's scholarship has received renewed attention due to the re-issuing of two of his major works: *The Psalms in Israel's Worship* (Eerdmans, 2004) and *He That Cometh* (Eerdmans, 2005). I have long been an avid reader of Mowinckel's works, and in 2002 I edited a small collection of his work on the prophets, *The Spirit and the Word: Prophecy and Tradition in Ancient Israel*, as part of the series I edited: Fortress Classics in Biblical Studies. That volume included his short monograph, *Prophecy and Tradition*, along with two additional articles.

One of the most intriguing aspects of Mowinckel's writing is his view to cross-cultural comparisons. Certainly Hermann Gunkel (with whom Mowinckel studied at Giessen) and his colleagues in history of religion research did this as well, especially with regard to other ancient literatures; but Mowinckel was also

Editor's Foreword

interested in the work being done by anthropologists, ethnologists, and phenomenologists of religion. Prior to World War I he had studied history of religions with Vilhelm Grønbech in Copenhagen.

One will note that throughout the present work Mowinckel heavily cites Gerardus van der Leeuw's *Phänomenologie der Religion* (ET: *Religion in Essence and Manifestation*). If the reader will compare Mowinckel's table of contents with that of van der Leeuw, it will be clear how much this foundational work influenced Mowinckel's volume. Other works that Mowinckel has drawn heavily upon are Johannes Pedersen, *Israel* (ET: *Israel: Its Life and Culture*); Efraim Briem, *På Trons Tröskel: Studier i Primitiv Religion* [On the Threshold of Faith: Studies in Primitive Religion]; Kaj Birket-Smith, *Kulturens Veje* (ET: *Paths of Culture: A General Ethnology*), Geo Widengren, *Religionens Värld: Religionsfenomenologiska Studier och Øversikter* [World Religions: Studies and Surveys in the Phenomenology of Religion]; as well as essays from *Lehrbuch des Religionsgeschichte* (4th ed., 1925) [Textbook on the History of Religion] and *Illustreret Religionshistorie* (2nd ed., 1948) [History of Religion Illustrated]. Mowinckel's interest in the present work is to draw on studies in the phenomenology of religion that will illuminate ancient Israel's expressions of their religious experience recorded in the Bible. As Nils Dahl, a former student of Mowinckel, summarizes:

> For practical reasons, but also as a matter of principle, Mowinckel did not base his representation upon a more or less comprehensive—and arbitrary—selection of material from all over the world, but concentrated on the manifestations of religion in Israel's life and history, under comparison with analogous aspects in other, mainly "primitive" and Near Eastern religions and Christianity. In agreement with Grønbech, and with an attitude that is much more common today than in the early decades of the century, he stressed that customs and ideas which appear to be very similar, take on a different character

Editor's Foreword

depending upon the total unit of culture and religion to which they belong.[1]

~

I have edited Fr. Sheehan's translation, mostly for English style and consistency. I have used the NRSV for biblical quotations, with some modifications. The bibliography contains all the works cited in the notes. Whenever English translations were available for the secondary literature, I have added the citations in brackets after Mowinckel's original citations. Furthermore, I have provided additional references in two ways: I have added a few citations in the notes (especially to Mowinckel's *The Psalms in Israel's Worship*, which had not yet been translated when this work was originally written) marked with [Ed.] for 'editor'; and I have added updated bibliographies for each chapter at the end of the book; these include works on the Bible as well as the phenomenology of religion. I have also provided bibliographies on Mowinckel's publications and evaluations of his work as well as indexes to ancient documents, subjects, and authors. I have provided the subtitle to clarify that Mowinckel's primary focus is the Old Testament, and not simply the phenomenology of religion in general.

I am grateful to the late John F. X. Sheehan, SJ, for his translation work; to Marquette University for their permission to use his work; and to the grandchildren of Sigmund Mowinckel, who gave their permission for this volume.

K. C. Hanson
February 1, 2012

---

1. Dahl, "Sigmund Mowinckel, Historian of Religion and Theologian," 18–19.

Abbreviations

ET	English translation
GTMMM	S. Michelet, Sigmund Mowinckel, and Nils Messel. *Det Gamle Testament*. 4 vols. Oslo: Aschenhoug, 1929–1955
NTT	*Norsk Teologisk Tidsskrift*
*RGG*²	*Die Religion in Geschechte und Gegenwart*. 2nd ed. Edited by Hermann Gunkel and Leopold Zscharnack. Tübingen: Mohr/Siebeck, 1927–1931

I. Religion and Its Manifestations

It has been said that religion occurs in three forms: as cult, myth, and ethics. One can state this in more ordinary Christian terms by saying: liturgy, the content of belief (doctrine), and the conduct of life (moral theology). It is not a question of three different disciplines within the world of religion but rather of three different manifestations. Each of these manifestations includes the other two in one way or another. Even if for purely practical reasons we divide these into three different "chapters" or "books" or "theological disciplines," nonetheless each is deeply involved with the others.

Perhaps this can be seen most clearly if one thinks of what "faith" means in Christianity. Faith embraces not only the assumption that particular ideas or concepts or confessions or doctrinal points are true, but it is also a life-determining existential thing, a relationship to the power that one "believes" in. To believe in God means not only to think or presume or to be convinced that God exists (for "even the demons do," James [2:19]), but it means also to build one's life on this conviction and behave according to it. It means to live with confidence in the God that one believes in and to guide oneself according to his will and his plan for the world and for oneself, and to serve him in this way. This also means seeking a personal relationship with God and accepting direction and strength, purpose and meaning from him; and it means spiritual and personal fellowship with all others who have this same relationship to God. It means, moreover, that one in this fellowship seeks a deeper relationship with God through prayers of petition and gratitude, listening and obedience. But this means, then, that belief embraces both "liturgy" and "ethical conduct." A Christian theology of faith or doctrine in its widest meaning also embraces a theology of the liturgy and moral theology or ethics. Both of these must receive their norms and their content in a way that is determined by the presentation of faith. The content of both ethics and liturgy depend on the ideas that one has about God, the way one believes in God.

Modern rationalism has had an inclination to regard the cult—liturgy and its forms—as something relatively unessential in religion. Certainly Protestantism has tended to stress doctrine so strongly that it has lost its appreciation of worship. It has been so preoccupied, moreover, with its role as witness to correct "spiritual," evangelical Christianity that it has looked down on liturgy with its "dead forms." Especially in the smaller Protestant sects this has been so. But in practice, those circles that are theoretically most opposed to cult have proved the strength of liturgy more strongly than the larger denominations have done. The smaller ones in reality felt and experienced the necessity for common liturgical gatherings in order to be "edified" in their godly lives. This edification encompasses not only the conservative mood and feelings one usually means by the word "edification." It has been repeatedly demonstrated that even the most "non-liturgical" denominations and groups quickly develop fixed forms for their worship services. Even if they call them "free meetings" or something similar, they very quickly develop what one would call a prescribed "ritual." The so-called "free" prayers in the "free" gatherings are as a rule strongly bound by tradition and habit with regard to content, form, and structure—indeed, often even inflection.

This meshes completely with the findings of recent research in comparative anthropology and religion. In fact, the more one learns not only about the so-called "primitive" religions, but also the older religions from "cultured" areas, the clearer it becomes that the most important thing for all of them was worship. Often there was more flexibility with regard to doctrine or confessions or concepts. The religion of the Old Testament—Israel's religion and the Judaism which developed from it—placed little store in doctrine but had very firm rules for liturgy. To participate in it properly was the chief duty of the believer. In later eras, as for example in apostolic Christianity, new forms are created and remain flexible for a while, but fixed forms develop very quickly. This need not be regarded as a decline or a loss of vitality. Rather, this process corresponds to a fundamental religious need and to a fundamental law of religion.

The comparative study of religion has also shown that there are in all religions fixed, basic forms or phenomena that occur repeatedly, even though there can be a broad spectrum of belief and content within any one of them. There is also a certain regularity with regard to the "elements" that make up cult. It is possible to set up a schema or pattern for liturgy, a phenomenology of worship, that at least in a purely formal way suits all religions, from the lowest up to Christianity. In all of them, prayers of petition and prayers of praise, "sacrifice" in some form or other, and certain rules of conduct, for example, play important roles even if the thought content and the religious or spiritual content of the prayers of the moral values inherent in the rules of conduct can be quite diverse.

All this shows that one confronts a rather important aspect of religion by viewing it from the perspective of cult. A comprehensible image of cult, for example, is very important for understanding the spiritual and religious content of the psalmic poetry that has arisen from the cult. Recent research, for example, has showed that psalms, and religious poetry generally, even in Christianity, originally came into existence in conjunction with the cult. A universal picture of the essence, forms, and content of cult is therefore also of value in order to understand the Christian religion.

But there is, of course, danger in setting up a universal schema of cult, namely that one may generalize and draw unjustified parallels between the phenomena and paint a picture, so to speak, that portrays everything and nothing. To be of value, such a comprehensive picture must comprise individual portrayals of the cult in each religion. These pictures must not be derived from universal schematized theories such as "animism," "pre-animism," "dynamism," "magic," and so forth, or from theories of evolutionary development. Rather, each should pay respect to the peculiarities of the particular religion in question and its inner structure. Every religion has its cardinal point from which its individual "phenomena," concepts, customs, and the like proceed and derive their meaning. If it is true anywhere, then it is in the world of religion that "two can say the same thing and still not say the same thing."

So when we try in the following to sketch a picture of religion and cult, or of cult as a manifestation of religion, then we shall try so far as possible to do that from a single concrete religion that is close to all of us and is a prelude to our own religion, namely the religion of Israel as it is available to us in the Old Testament. But we shall also try to show that we are dealing here with a certain manifestation of something universal and make use of other material to the extent that it can shed light on that of the Old Testament.

2 | The Meaning of Cult

Cultus is the Latin word for worship. The word actually means work. It is also used, for example, if one "works" (cultivates) a field, or engages in other types of activity.

The corresponding Hebrew root (*'bd*) has to do with "service" and the verb *'abad* "serve" or "slave for" and so forth is used for a slave who serves a master, the beast of burden that "toils," the farmer who "works" or cultivates the soil, and the person who serves, worships, and obeys God.

We should ask now which of these aspects lies behind the cultic meaning. Within the Old Testament, at any rate, it is clear that the cultic meaning of the word is older than the more universal religious meaning: to stand in a relationship of faith and obedience to the deity; to serve a deity means primarily to take part in that deity's cult, to stand in a cultic relationship toward that deity.

It has been asserted that there can be cult without any relationship to personal gods. Work then would characterize the tending of a power that is useful for the life and wellbeing of people (see below). It has been pointed out, for example, that the personal gods of the Australian Aborigines are cultic objects only to a slight degree. Their cultic rites, their *korrobori* (animal dances) and so forth are really efficacious ceremonies that serve to increase the animals on which they depend (the food ceremony), or the power of the animal totem. It has also been pointed out that Buddhism was originally a religion without any relationship to personal gods. Yet it is questionable whether such "cultivating" of "power" has ever taken place without a concept that there was a personal being behind the power. A purely "objective" or "rational" (in the primitive sense of the word) "cultivating" in order to guide power to wherever it is needed can hardly be called religious, if indeed it has ever occurred. We must also remember that our distinction between personal and impersonal beings is modern and has little to do with "primitive" ways of thought (see below). For them, an animal also has its "personality," its "being" with its characteristics; and an object has its soul and is compared with humans. It is "realistic," from the viewpoint of primitive thought, when fairytales permit animals, plants, and objects—a sword or the earth and so forth—to speak, to feel, and to think. In Australian aboriginal rites, the totem animal or plant and the holy, power-filled object represent the deity. And as far as Buddhism is concerned, it was originally a purely philosophical and intellectual path of salvation; but as soon as it became religious, personal gods entered into it. Buddha himself became a god of salvation.

In any case, the Old Testament term "service," meaning worship in the cult, is always related to the concept of a more powerful personal being toward whom the cult exercises its service. It is conceivable that in an older, prehistoric phase of the religious life of the Hebrews or Semites they believed that this "service" was also a "tending" or "cultivating" that the particular deity needed and that gave him greater power and ability to be the god of those who worshiped him. Traces of such antecedent ideas are found also in Israel, as we shall see later. But that does not change the fact that in the cult we are dealing with a relationship between worshippers and a personal being who is worshipped. In fact, the very religious inclination toward "someone" on whom humans in one or another way are dependent is a chief characteristic of the cult and an essential moment in it.

In the cult, humanity is dealing with a "someone" who must be "served" and possibly even taken care of, whom one has a need of, and to whom one must subordinate oneself in one way or another—someone who in this way comes into contact with

The Meaning of Cult

and maintains a relationship with the worshippers and offers them access to him.

In view of all this, we have good reason to accept Evelyn Underhill's definition of cult or worship as "the response of the creature to the Eternal,"[1] the answer to a call, to an address by the eternal.

In a purely formal way, cult can be defined as the visible forms that a society establishes and arranges by which the religious experience and fellowship between deity and the religious group—the association with and worship of the divine—takes place.[2] That is to say, it is set in motion, comes to expression and attains its goal. And we can expand this a bit. It embraces all of the perceptible activities repeated at certain times and especially in certain places and bound to a holy tradition both in ritual and in word. These are performed on behalf of the society by representatives appointed and prepared for the task. Its intention is in this way to come into union with the sacred forces and thus to create, strengthen, and renew those life values on which the community's life and prosperity depend. Cult also testifies that this relationship between the deity and humans has been attained and indeed functions. Again, looking from the formal side, one can see that four things belong to cult. These are ritual or a fixed way of proceeding, symbolic representations of the reality or the realities involved, sacraments or sacramental words and actions, and sacrifices offered in one or another form.[3] Later on we shall examine all of these elements in more detail.

---

1. Underhill, *Worship*, 3: "Worship in all its grades and kinds, is the response of the creature to the Eternal." See also Will, *Le Culte*, 22: "Every religion requires a cultic form. Every cult establishes a religious foundation and a religious inspiration."

2. For the cultic idea, see van der Leeuw, *Phänomenologie*, 317ff. [ET: *Religion in Essence and Manifestation*, 339-458]; Widengren, *Religionens Värld*, 162ff., 204ff.; Lehmann "Erscheinungs- und Ideenwelt der Religion," 87ff.; Pfister, "Kultus" (much schematized, by Bertholet, "Kultus"). For the sources of cult in this book, see Mowinckel, *Psalmenstudien*, II:19-35; also Mowinckel, "Drama"; Quell, *Das kultische Problem der Psalmen*, 18ff. [Ed.: see also Mowinckel, *The Psalms in Israel's Worship*, 1:1-22.]

3. Cf. Underhill, *Worship*, 18ff.

3 | The Magical Perception of Reality

FORMS OF THE CULT DERIVED FROM A PERCEPTION OF REALITY

The forms in which fellowship in the cult occurs are dependent on and shaped not only by a particular religion's view of God, the world, and humanity, but also by its entire perception of reality and way of thought. Stated briefly, it is effected by a total concept of existence and by all of the individual perceptions about the important matters of life that a particular time or group of people has.

A view of reality depends on a particular people's relationship to nature and the culture through which it has been formed. Hence, it is natural that we begin with the oldest, so called "primitive" cultures. We do this because these stand closer to that reality that is immediately available (nature) than do the later urban or national cultures, and because they are "closed," i.e., all-embracing and unified so that religion permeates the whole. In them, there is no gap between believing and knowing or between the supernatural and the natural. There is, in a certain sense, a harmonious unity of culture.

Within these cultures, one can distinguish between three chief types, each of which has its corresponding type of religion and cult. The types are the herding culture, the hunting culture, and the farming culture.[1] Cult takes a different form in a culture that relies on the buffalo, for example, than in one that requires the fertility and blessing of field or of domesticated animals. The

---

1. Cf. Briem, *På Trons Tröskel*, 77ff.

The Magical Perception of Reality

tribes of Israel before their immigration were a people who generally lived in a patriarchal herding and military culture. More precisely, they were semi-nomads who tended small domesticated animals. After their migration, they settled in an agricultural land and consequently took over its forms of culture and cult. This tension between Israelites and Canaanites determined Israel's religious, spiritual, and social history. Nevertheless, the two cultures shared certain essential traits and phenomena in their religious and cultic lives that were bound to the same perception of reality. It is an acknowledged fact that worship is one of the most conservative of human activities. One sees in all religions, therefore—even in Christianity—that it contains elements derived from earlier and now abandoned perceptions of life and religion. Their original significance has been partially forgotten, yet they survive because they have received new meanings. Perhaps it would be more accurate to say that they had to take on new meanings because the conservative power of the cult keeps them alive.

In Israel's cult this was also the case. This is due to the fact that Israel's religion and Judaism have had a long history that during the passage of time has caused many important changes in the religion itself. The religion of the prophets was not simply the same as that of Moses or the patriarchs, and Judaism differs in many ways from the religion of ancient Israel and its cult. The official religious leaders at the time of the prophets—the priests and the temple personnel—did not view religion and cult the same way the prophets themselves did.

Hence, the cult of Israel has always—certainly during the classical period when the psalms were composed—contained many elements that can be understood only as part of the mindset of an older time with its perception of reality and its religious concepts.

The most ancient Israel had a perception of reality and a mind-set that we call primitive. It has also been called pre-logical[2] or pre-rational or mystical. All of these terms are applicable. By primitive perception of reality we mean not only the first disorganized—and for us often incomprehensible, unfamiliar and, therefore, unreasonable—beginnings of human thought, but rather a coherent mind-set reflecting a oneness with nature.[3] This holds true not only for the culture of the ostensibly uncultured Australian Aborigines and the Botocudo tribe of Brazil,[4] but also for the highly developed cultures of the ancient Near East. They too were built upon this primitive perception of reality, even if it underwent a special form of development in many directions that gave it a rational mind-set in some respects and laid the foundation for a scholarly perception of reality, just as Greek philosophy did. This foundation developed into the modern perception of reality with the principle of causality as its foundation.

THE MAGICAL OR MYTHICAL PERCEPTION OF REALITY

Central to the primitive perception of reality is the magical view. This word is often used in a misleading way. One often perceives magic partially as a prelude to religion,[5] partially as something

---

2. The expression in that of Levy-Bruhl, as for example in *Les fonctions mentales dans les societies inferieures* [ET: *How Natives Think*]; and Levy-Bruhl, *La mythologie primitive* [ET: *Primitive Mythology*]. On this question see Albright, *From Stone Age to Christianity*, 84, 123–24; and Albright, *Archaeology and the Religion of Israel*, 25ff. "The mythical mind-set" is what Moltke Moe calls this, with special attention to its formation in epic myths and in mythical presentations. See his *Mai og Minne* in Samlede Skrifter, 2:265ff. Cf. Ankermann, "Die Religion der Naturvolker," 131ff; Nilsson, *Primitive Religion*; Nilsson, *Primitive Kultur*; Karsten, *Naturfolkens religion*; Lehman, *Religionens Värld*; Frankfort, et al., *The Intellectual Adventure of Ancient Man*.

3. Cf. Grønbech, *Primitive Religion*, and his article in *Illustreret Religionshistorie*, 2nd ed., 11ff., and especially 54ff.

4. The expression is that of Weule; see his *Kultur der Kulturlosen*.

5. That the magical influence of impersonal powers through automatic magical words and rites was a "pre-stage" from which religion has evolved was a strongly asserted thesis of the older generation of historians of religion, with Tylor and Frazer as the pioneering authorities. See Frazer's major work, *The*

that is more or less identical with sorcery and as a corrupt competitor of religion. Both of these are incorrect. Magic in and of itself has nothing to do with religion, whether as a prelude or as a corruption. The magical view and its concrete form (magic) is not a kind of religion but a view of reality, a particular way of understanding things and the relationships between them. It is a *Weltanschauung* (worldview). This *Weltanschauung*, corresponds in fact to the view of reality that modern people try to formulate on the basis of the law of causality or concern for causal contexts just as physics, chemistry, biology, and psychology attempt to discover them. To this extent anyway, Frazer was correct when he saw in magic the primitive attempt to establish science.

Peculiar to the magical or mythical perception of reality is that it does not distinguish, as we do, between inanimate and animate, between organic and inorganic. All have "power" and "life" of one kind or another in them. This can also be expressed by saying that all things have a "soul." For the ancient Israelites, there was no doubt that animals had "souls," just as human beings do. We must be aware, however, that to the ancient Israelites soul was not set in opposition to "body." They were not anthropological dualists. A body equipped with "life spirit" is described as "a living soul" in the Old Testament (Gen 2:7). It is this idea about "life" and "soul" in things that has given rise to the erroneous theory of animism as a universal prelude in the history of religion. Such is the origin of the idea, also erroneous, that one distinguishes between "animatism" ("pre-animism"), which has to do with impersonal power or the "source of life" in things, and "animism," which has to do with a soul.

The primitive view of reality distinguishes neither between power and matter nor between material and immaterial. To ancient Israel it was obvious that even "spirit" was a fine material thing (the Hebrew word *ruach* means wind, air, and "spirit"). It was much finer and more powerful than flesh. Even "life" was

---

Golden Bough. Widengren has correctly opposed this superficial "evolutionism"; see his *Religionens Ursprung*.

material. "Life (or: soul) is in the blood," according to a Hebrew truism (Gen 9:4; Lev 17:11, 14).

There was, then, no sharp boundary between personal and impersonal as has been pointed out above. Primitive thought, therefore, had little difficulty in personifying the various aspects of a being: its properties, its activities, or even parts of a body. The ancient world could perceive these as semi-independent essences (hypostases). Certainly, this was true in the world of the gods. For the ancient Semites, justice and judgment became personal, independent, divine essences, and the Israelites could speak in about the same way about Yahweh's justice and judgment. At bottom, there was no distinction either between the living and the dead. The dead could be assigned the same feelings and actions and reactions as the living. Although for the ancient Israelites the dead person was "one without power," he still had in recompense another kind of strength. He was the "knowing one" and a "divine being," and could therefore be invoked to give oracles, as we read in the narrative about Saul and the sorceress at Endor (1 Sam 28:3–25).

A salient feature of primitive peoples' thinking is that they thought in totalities. Today, we isolate concepts from one another and then reassemble them in artificial, abstract, "universal ideas." We classify them. The concepts of primitive peoples are all-embracing totalities that tend to overlap one another and only reflect the whole from a different viewpoint. If we were to ask an ancient Israelite to distinguish between Yahweh's justice and Yahweh's covenant fidelity, this would seem to him an idiotic question. What we call wholes or parts are for primitives two sides of the same reality. They do not distinguish, for example, between the nation or the tribe and the individual. In the individual the totality is manifested. The ancestors live in their descendants. For the Israelite prophet, the contemporary generation that he addressed was "that whole generation which I (i.e., Yahweh) led out from Egypt."

The Magical Perception of Reality

Another characteristic is therefore that which has been called "mythic participation." All parts of the totality share in the full essence of the totality; or, to put it better, the fullness of being is present to the same degree both in the whole and in all of its parts. A person's "life" or "soul" or "power" is at the same time present in that person and in everything that belongs to him or her: hair, bones after death, etc. It is even in one's clothes or weapons to some degree, or the total force of one's essence can be concentrated in these things. In a king's crown or scepter all of his royalty can be present as his authority and heroism.

This holds too for the relationship between the community and the individual. In the "essence" or "soul" or "power" of the social totality or its "well-being," all individuals have a portion, and this "essence" can at certain important times be concentrated in an individual person who represents the whole as a chief, a king, or a seer-priest. This totality is the reality that manifests itself more or less completely in the individual. "Israel" is such an eternally existing totality that actualizes its essence both in the ancestors and in the individual historical representations of the nation and in its individual members. The task of the individual is to actualize this essence, to represent the Israelite "type" here and now. We can get some idea about what this is when we think of Plato's doctrine of "ideas." For him, they were reality. That this doctrine has something in common with primitive or mythic perceptions of reality is obvious.

Relationship, "common bone and blood," can be formed just as genuinely through the ritual formation of a covenant as through natural procreation and birth (see Gen 2:23; 2 Sam 5:1; 19:12). One can, therefore, speak of "identification" as characteristic of the mythical mind-set. That which resembles a person or a thing has commonality with it in kind and essence and can represent it. A picture of a person is a person and can represent him or her with full "reality." A person, a deity, a human being, or an institution can be totally represented by a symbol that has one or another likeness with the particular reality. To us it may seem that just about anything can be a symbol for just about anything. But it is not so to primitive peoples. They see a likeness and a context and a correspondence of essence where we do not see them, and there is always a thought in their symbols. We speak of "only" a symbol. The mythic process of thought sees the reality in the symbol. In a mythic way, it is the thing or the person. It shares in the person's "essence." If one does something magical to another's clothes, hair, or a picture, those actions happen to that person.[6]

What we call abstract ideas are for the mythical mind-set concrete realities. "Honor" and "shame" are not something attributed to the estimation of a person, but they are objective properties in the person himself, an aspect of his positive or negative force. "Fortune" is also a property of the person. To the Israelites, soul and honor were synonymous ideas. This is also true of the notion of "name," which expresses or includes the personality of a thing itself with its characteristic essence. In an object that in one way or another is like something else, primitives see a real representation of one thing that is identical with another. They see symbols everywhere and interpret them

---

6. I wish to stress this view of "magic" and its relationship to religion. It does not coincide with the traditional view and does not appear, as far as I can see, clearly in any of the more recent efforts to clarify the problem. Perhaps it is closest to van der Leeuw's understanding of the problem in his *Phänomenologie*, 516ff. [ET: *Religion in Essence and Manifestation*, 543–54]. For the notion and its discussion, see also ibid., 5 [ET: 24–26], and the index s.v. "magie" [ET: "magic"]; Widengren, *Religionens Värld*, 9ff.; and Widengren, *Religionens Ursprung*, 28ff; Chantepie de la Saussaye, ed., *Lehrbuch*, s.v. "Magie, magisches"; Wetter, *Religion och Magie*, 289ff.; Mowinckel, *Psalmenstudien*, V:14–18 (excursus), and my review of Widengren's *Religionens Värld* (1946). Birkeli, in his *Religionshistorie*, 1:234ff., appears to promote the same view as this author: magic among the primitive corresponds to applied science among us. But it is misleading to say, as Birkeli does, that magic "consists in canceling natural causes and producing effects that stand in connection with causes only by arbitrary thought patterns." For the primitive, the connections that magic sets into motion and then uses are as natural and real as our principles of causality. For them the discussion here is of the real, not "arbitrary," thought patterns.

The Magical Perception of Reality

as such representations. They "think in symbols." We assert that they see real contexts through "the association of ideas." The same thing is done today by many humanistic scholars. What we call a symbolic action is a reality for this mind-set. If some action or other is performed in a more or less symbolic play, a primitive drama, these events happen. They become a reality in and with what is enacted. In a war dance, for example, the enemy suffers a defeat—an imaginary one, we would say. The successful outcome of the hunt is assured by the fact that the detection, pursuit, and defeat of the wild animal are acted out beforehand.

It is sometimes said that primitive peoples do not recognize causal connections between things. This does not mean that existence is devoid of connection and chaotic for them; on the contrary, there is a mythic and real connection and inner activity between everything that exists. Even primitive peoples can make observations and draw conclusions about cause and effect. But they do not see them from a physical or chemical viewpoint. Any coincidence of events, therefore, can appear to them in the context of cause. Their law of causality, so to speak, works both ways. What may be an effect for us can also be a cause for them. From their observations and experiences they can think just as strictly logically as we can; but their interpretation of the starting points or the contexts differs from our own. We distinguish between technology and magic, but they do not, because they know contexts other than those of physics or chemistry. They know, for example, that the "soul" and "spirit" are realities. We chide them because they think and work "magically." For them, however, that is just as natural and as technological as all the laws of technology and nature are for us. Their apparently meaningless and irrational magical activities are for them logical and rational consequences of their view of reality and of the essence and context of things.[7]

---

7. For the different types of magical actions (image magic, homeopathic magic, sympathetic magic, etc., a typology in which I have no great interest), see Birkeli, *Religionshistorie*, 1:234ff.

TOTEMISM

Much more of interest could be said about the primitive, magical view of reality and mind-set,[8] but this will have to suffice. One widespread phenomenon connected with it must be mentioned, namely totemism, which occurs in North America, Australia, and Africa.[9] The kernel of totemism is that it involves a close, mysterious connection between a tribe, a clan, and so forth—or an individual person—and a certain animal or plant that is the totem for a particular group. (Totem is a North American Indian word.) The group and the animal or plant have a common mythic ancestor, and each exemplar of this species is "brother" to the particular group of persons and its individual members. The bear, for example, is father and brother to every member of the bear clan. The totem fathers and the totem essences are the protectors of the group and its members whose well-being and power the group is dependent on. These ideas can be developed into a rather complicated social system that, for example, can determine which totem groups can enter into marriage with others and which cannot. Even lifeless objects can be regarded as totems. The individual can have one's own special totem. It is important for the totem-group to have efficacious rituals that increase the prosperity of the totem on which the group is dependent. Such ceremonies are especially known among the Australian Aborigines.

---

8. A more detailed presentation can be found in Levy-Bruhl, *Les fonctions mentales dans les societies inferieures* [ET: *How Natives Think*]. Levy-Bruhl, however, sees the matter from the outside, or from above. See also the lucid presentation in Birket-Smith, *Kulturens Veje*, 2:153ff. [ET: *Paths of Culture*]. Birket-Smith's opinion that the origin of religion is to be sought in this mind-set is untenable, and his distinction between cult and magic is unsatisfactory; see ibid., 2:149ff.

9. Birket-Smith, *Kulturens Veje*, 2:42ff. [ET: *Paths of Culture*]; Briem, *På Trons Tröskel*, 99ff., 265ff; van der Leeuw, *Phänomenologie*, 60ff. [ET: *Religion in Essence and Manifestation*, 78–82].

The Magical Perception of Reality

POWER OR MANA

The magical view is more than a *Weltanschauung* (worldview). It is not simply a theoretical outlook, but a practical relationship to that surrounding reality, which is the world in which the primitive peoples live and of which they are an integral part. The magical view of reality, then, is not abstract science, but rather applied science. It is an attitude toward reality that is practical in its intent and effect. In that respect, it is something universal, eternally valid, and necessary, even for modern peoples. The magical action is, therefore, not what we would call a technique. Rather, it is the reaction of a personal will that, together with external means, marshals all the forces of the soul to shaping reality, the world, so that it can be lived in.[10] The magical view is part of the human desire to rule the reality that surrounds one and on which one depends.

In that which should be ruled, there must be order and a regular process, and it must be subject to deliberate and orderly activity by the one who would rule. This magical view, to be sure, thinks not in terms of physical or chemical causalities, but rather of forces and influences embracing all that we would call material, spiritual, and supernatural. For primitive peoples, all these are one. Perhaps they are more correct here than contemporary scholarship is willing to see. They comprehend reality in a natural analogy with themselves and assume that the surrounding world can be ruled and used according to the same "laws" that they see governing themselves and their spiritual life.

They note in themselves forces and impulses that rise and fall. They see how their own imagination, lust, and will are set into motion through the sight of the eye, an odor that reaches the nostrils, or a taste and can then become an irresistible desire, "a power." They can be influenced by words and tones that swell in them. Physical hunger and sexual desire can give them enormous strength. They remark that all these things work on and

---

10. See van der Leeuw, *Phänomenologie*, 515ff. [ET: *Religion in Essence and Manifestation*, 557–58].

are worked on by something in them, an "I," which is that person and yet at the same time not really that person. It is simultaneously both the subject and the object of their experience.

This "I" is constantly in union with a "thou" or with many "thous" in a thousand different ways. Mysterious ribbons and threads bind them together and pull them apart. They give an experience of fullness and growth or of fear and defeat. A human "soul" is power, wields power, and is influenced by power. Everywhere there are relationships, either mysterious or patent, apparently "rational" or incomprehensible; but in everything there is one or another kind of power, useful or harmful, good or evil. The will is power.

The magical view of reality thus means that everything in existence is made up of mysterious powers and strengths that are externalized through things or phenomena. Everything that exists has some degree of such power[11] or *mana*, the Melanesian word by which it is called. It is not a question of one simple, impersonal, common power in existence like electricity, but rather of many kinds of power or abilities that can be perceived as more or less impersonal, as a quality regarded as a kind of energy, or it can be more or less personified as spirits (animism). The difference between these two ways of perceiving are for primitive peoples much less important and much less essential than they are for us, and the boundaries between these conceptions are, therefore, flexible.[12] There are many types of power. The warrior has his; the woman in labor has hers; the horse has its. There is a great power and a lesser power. It is a sign that the primitive mind-set is on the point of disintegrating and being rationalized

---

11. Cf. ibid., 3ff.; Söderblom, *Gudstrons Uppkomst*, 30ff.; Marett, *The Threshold of Religion*, 128ff.

12. There is, therefore, no reason to set up such an "evolutionistic" schema, as the older scholars of religion often did, with a universal development from animatism (belief in life or power), to animism, to belief in demons, and later to belief in God. All of this is artificially schematized, as Widengren has rightly opposed in his *Religionens Värld*; but he makes some exaggerations of his own in the opposite direction. See also Benedict, *Patterns of Culture*.

when "power" is attributed only to gods or demons. Power can be concentrated in individual parts of the body such as the blood, heart, kidneys, liver, marrow, genitals, or hair;[13] but it can also manifest itself in everything that one has and that the powerful person uses, such as clothing, weapons, and so forth.

All of these powers and abilities influence one another or can be brought to do so by various practices and measures. The one who has great power can subordinate the power of others to oneself and use it for one's own advantage. Power can be increased or lessened. This is evident in the lifecycle of nature. That there is power in human beings or in animals, in stones and in weapons, is something that everyone can experience. The same holds true for intoxicating beverages and food. But also that there is power in the word. Everyone can certainly experience how the powerful word or most of all the powerful song can bring a whole mass of people to act as a unit, how the right word can subject one person to another, or how a person by the power of a word can attain something that he or she wants. We distinguish in this area a psychological action from a physical. For primitive peoples, all of this is "power," and a dualistic distinction between corporeal (material) and spiritual is completely foreign to them.

TABU

Power is of many kinds, and it is mysterious and sometimes unaccountable. It makes the soil produce and causes trees to give fruit. But the power of poisonous plants kills and a stone in a cliff can suddenly reveal its power by rolling down and killing someone. So it is important to understand power in order to be able to deal with it correctly, to use it, and to take care of it. It must be handled properly. If something is filled with power, in

---

13. We find the same thought among the ancient Israelites. The "life" or "soul" is in the blood (Gen 9:4; Lev 17:10–14) as a person's life-force. "Life goes out from the heart" (Prov 7:23). The liver, the "heaviness" (*kabed*), is a person's gravity, that is to say "honor" (*kabod*). For Samson the strong man, the seat of his dedicated strength was in his hair (Judg 16:17).

many ways and under certain circumstances, it is forbidden, or *tabu*, to use the Polynesian word by which it is usually known in the phenomenology of religion. It is like a sign that says "Danger: High Voltage." Rules arise, therefore, for dealing with power. All of these tabu rules are grounded in the magical perception of reality.[14] They can be extremely diverse. For example, this or that kind of food or this or that action can be tabu for one person while something else is for another. That which an ordinary person cannot do the "skilled" person—such as the medicine man, the shaman, or the priest—can do. Something is tabu at certain times and something else at other times. Certain times or days can be tabu, either for certain kinds of activity or for all kinds of work. Especially widespread is the derived notion that the four phases of the moon are holy and unsuitable for work. That was the case, for example, in Babylonia. That was also how the Sabbath originated. The word actually meant the day of the full moon. But it was later extended to cover all four days making the phases of the moon and finally was separated completely from the moon and became the seventh day in any ordinary week.

THE VIEW OF REALITY IN PRACTICAL LIFE: MAGIC

Power and powers can, as we have said, influence one another. It can be set into motion or be exploited or used for a purpose. Existence is so arranged that things influence one another. To this magical perception of reality belongs the idea that where there is likeness, there is common essence. The whole can be in a part. All of an animal's power can be in its tooth or claw or heart. Words can influence persons, things, or relationships because there is power in them. By imitating the splashing of rain, one can make it rain. By igniting fire, one can make the sun strong again. By destroying an image of another, one can destroy that person.[15] It is this idea of a more or less systematic, mutual influ-

14. Cf. van der Leeuw, *Phänomenologie*, 23ff. [ET: *Religion in Essence and Manifestation*, 43–51]; Briem, *På Trons Tröskel*, 61ff.

15. Cf. Ankermann "Die Religion der Naturvolker," 145ff.

ence of powers and objects that is the essence of the magical view of reality, and it is this view of reality carried out in practice that one calls magic.[16]

As an applied art and activity, magic is rooted in the wish and the desire to rule over the varieties of power and strength and to exploit them to the advantage of the community's life and prosperity. In any event, it is intended to balance as well as possible all the dangerous, competing powers. Power in itself is ethically as indifferent as electricity. It can both help and harm. It can make seeds grow or shatter a house with a burst of lightning. It can create and kill; it can be used for good or evil.[17] "Wisdom" is knowing as much as possible about these powers and the means of ruling—or at least directing—them. The art of life is to use them for one's own good and to employ them as a defense against enemies and to destroy their power.

By using all efficacious means, then, the skilled person tries to influence power or powers and to exploit them through powerful words and manipulations of many kinds. Most of these efforts represent a kind of symbolic imagery. Through certain imitative actions and corresponding words, the person presents the effect he or she wishes to attain and believes that is thereby achieved. Earlier we cited two examples: sprinkling water in order to call forth rain and igniting a fire in order to give the sun new power. Every rational primitive person has some skill in dealing with power. Every farmer must know how power in the soil and the seed and the livestock should be used and increased. But when it comes to more difficult or unusual things, such as lightning, thunder, rain, war, sickness, and the like, a chosen class of specialists (of "scholars") takes over. Modern ignorance of this

---

16. The connection between magic and *mana*-belief is also stressed by Birkeli, *Religionshistorie*, 1:246ff.

17. This ethical indifference toward power is clear among the Australian Aborigines, where the mighty and skilled medicine man indiscriminately uses his power to harm a personal enemy in his own clan, or to kill the enemy or transgressor. Cf. Briem, *På Trons Tröskel*, 149ff.

was a bit wiser than it realized when it coined the generic term "medicine man" for these specialists in magic.

SORCERY

On the other hand, the constant use of "magic" and "sorcery" as synonyms is indeed misleading. Sorcery is the use of magical wisdom to the harm of the community or to achieve purely egoistic ends. All primitive peoples condemn sorcery, and most primitive societies with a little more advanced organization have strict laws against it. It was not only Paul and late Israelite legislation that forbade sorcery; even the Sumerian King Gudea of Lagash boasted in his inscriptions that he had driven all of the sorcerers and witches out of his domain.[18]

Since power is ethically indifferent, it can be used for good or evil, for benefit or harm. One needs to be both skilled and well-intentioned to handle power properly to the advantage of others, that is, one's own community. The community, therefore, has authorized users of power: the chief, the priest, the shaman, and so forth. But power can also fall into the hands of the wrong people and be used improperly to the harm of the group as, for example, when the wise men of the enemies use it, or a personal foe uses it to violate law and propriety. Power and its use then becomes sorcery or satanism or damnation.[19]

There are beings, demons, and people who are full of such sorcery or evil power; they are what the Israelites called the "evil ones" (*rešaʿim*), the crooked, the twisted, the harmful, the traitors, or quite simply sinners—those who had excluded them-

---

18. 1 Sam 28:3; Cylinder A of Gudea, 13, 14ff. See Thureau-Dangin, *Die sumerisch-akkadischen Konigsinschriften*, 102ff.

19. Cf. Mowinckel, *Psalmenstudien*, III:68ff. The general distinction between "white" and "black" magic is a theological product of the Middle Ages, in other words of scholarly thought about magic, and that is valid enough in so far as it understands that there was a magical art and insight that could also be used for sorcery. This distinction is unsatisfactory as scholarly terminology, for it obscures the difference between religion and magic. The misleading use of "sorcery" as a synonym for a magical view and practice is blurred also in the work of Birket-Smith, *Kulturens Veje*, 2:149ff. [ET: *Paths of Culture*, 358–78].

selves from the community. Evil words, evil wishes, evil gossip, the evil eye, derision, and contempt are effective means of doing harm because they are full of such evil power.[20] The Israelites, like all other primitive peoples, regarded not only the magical power of the enemy but also their religion and worship, their gods and demons, as evil powers, and they considered their priests to be sorcerers.[21] Especially when a religion becomes exclusive, as Israel's increasingly did, everything that belongs to foreign religions comes under its condemnation.

In Hebrew there is a vivid example of this differentiation between "power" and "powers." One word (*'on*) means power, especially human or reproductive power. Another word (*'awon*) means harm, the doing of harm, the means of harming, misfortune, and so forth, especially sorcery, satanism, the power of sorcery, or the means and action and the misfortune that result from all that. But both *'on* and *'awon* go back originally to an older word *'un*, which meant power (*mana*) in a universal sense. The distinction between the good and the evil use of power has led to a corresponding differentiation of the originally neutral word.[22]

In such a distinction between kinds of power lies, so to speak, the term of a moral and religious distinction between good and holy power and its use on one hand, and sorcery or satanism on the other. Medieval theology hit the nail on the head: in religion and cult one is dealing with God's holy power, but in sorcery, with that of the devil.

---

20. Cf. Pedersen, *Israel*, I–II:430–32.
21. Isa 41:29; 66:3; Amos 5:5; 2 Kgs 9:22; Isa 12:15; 47:9.
22. See Mowinckel, *Psalmenstudien* I, where sometimes the understanding of individual point goes too far.

4 | Magic and Religion

As we noted above, modern scholars have often suggested that religion developed from magic. This is out of the question because magic and religion, in and of themselves, are dimensions of two distinct essences and are therefore incomparable. A religion cannot evolve from a *Weltanschauung*. The most that can come from such an origin is a surrogate for religion; but no surrogate can evolve into something genuine any more than a dandelion root can develop into coffee.[1] Magic, as we have seen, is the ex-

---

[1] It is not right, therefore, to say as van der Leeuw does, that "magic is religion" (*Phänomonologie*, 519 [ET: *Religion in Essence and Manifestation*, 547]). Religion occurs only when it is put into connection with "the holy" and with the deity. Then even magic is made holy. After one has recognized that magic and religion are different, and therefore incommensurable things, the useless efforts carried on by an evolutionistic viewpoint to distinguish between them and to determine their "essence" in connection with one another disappear. The usual definition is based in one way or another on the view that in magic one is dealing with "impersonal" powers and a mechanical control of the natural world by automatic rites and words, or with a compulsion of ritual and speech over things and demons and gods, while religion presupposes free, personal gods who can be influenced by gifts, sacrifices, and prayers to help by their own volition. See Lehmann's "Erscheinungs- und Ideenwelt der Religion," 87; Nilsson, *Primitive Religion*, 10, 71. It is more correct to say religion is "piety" where the supernatural in relationship to humans is subject, while in magic it is object (Wetter, *Religion och Magi*). As a rule, the statement of the problem and further discussion are obscured because people have mixed magic and sorcery together, just as these expressions go together in popular usage, and in many modern languages the two things are not distinguished. A fundamental criticism of all these efforts is given by Wetter, *Religion och magi*, 289ff. Wetter's criticism affects his own effort, however, because he has started out from the same evolutionistic schema as the others. Cf. Mowinckel, *Psalmenstudien*, V:14–18 (Excursus).

pression of an all-embracing view of reality and as such forms the background for the oldest religion or the framework in which it developed, but it is not a prelude to or a root of religion. It is true that religion and magic touch one another and have often done so, with the result that the religion has degenerated into magic.[2] When this happens, magic suppresses that which is truly "religious" in religion: piety and respect for "the holy." Then the liturgical rites and all kinds of obscure formulas become impious ways of compelling even the gods. The deity itself becomes a means in the skilled hand. Then all of those elements that have been defeated and pushed into the background emerge from the cult or the magic of a primitive people once again in the boundary of religion and grow over that boundary. This happened, for example, in the later stages of the Egyptian religions and in Taoism in China. Since every religion and its forms of expression is determined by the perception of reality in which the worshippers live, it is inevitable that the forms of the oldest religions contain much that is founded in a view of reality that is magical and is stamped by the practice of magic.[3] But that does not have its origin in the essence of religion.

There is one thing that magic has in common with religion and especially with religion as cult, namely that both seek to bring about effects that people themselves cannot create through their normal activities and abilities. "If magic means an action with an intended supernatural effect, then every cultic rite contains an element of magic. Thus, we can speak of religious magic but not of magical religion," according to Brede Kristensen.[4] And we can add that if magic also contains an element of personally willed and formed approach to reality, then it holds true for religion and religious cultic action to an even greater degree. Each in its own way is the expression of an attitude toward reality that is more real and more in agreement with laws of life than any theoretical

---

2. Cf. Albright, *From Stone Age to Christianity*, 139.
3. Cf. Birkeli, *Religionshistorie*, I:248ff.
4. Kristensen, *Tro eller Overtro*, 35.

view of a spectator. Religion exists when this positive approach to life confronts a living god—however inadequate its understanding of this god's essence may be.

The thought that cult is derivative, in one or another way, from magic resounds also in the distinction between the two types of cult—those in which the supernatural power is encountered purely as a dynamic entity, and those in which it is personal or theistic.[5] This distinction is a false abstraction, however, for there is no sharp boundary between the "dynamic" and the "theistic" concepts of powers and gods. The distinction personal/impersonal is on the whole modern and does not reflect ancient peoples' way of thinking. What is correct about the theory is that religion on its lowest levels is much more permeated by a magical perception of reality. But depending partly on whether this yields to or is penetrated by a more rational view and partly on whether the religion progresses and becomes conscious of its own peculiarity, the magical content recedes. This means that the religion becomes bound together with another view of existence and that the truly religious element in the religion—the conviction about and the relationship to a personal, volitional God who of his own desire enters into union with humanity—emerges on a clearer and more conscious level. The history of revelation is also the history of religion's liberation from magic both in theory and in practice. But this does not hinder, as we have said, a religion from dragging along with it many remnants of a magical mind-set or degenerating so that the magical overcomes the truly religious.

In religion, humanity is encountered or summoned by something above it; and when humanity responds to that summons and submits to it in feeling, will, and action a reality and power is formed that determines, uplifts, and renews life. In magic, humanity orients itself to itself as the starting point toward the mysterious yet rational reality that surrounds it and seeks to influence and form that reality according to its needs.

---

5. Cf. A. Bertholet, "Kultus."

Magic and Religion

The theory that religion developed from a kind of pre-religious, magical stage often takes the form that cult must be the origin of religion. Some people regard as cult all of the efforts that people with primitive perceptions of reality made in order to come into contact with the power or to influence it to their advantage. But not all such actions are cultic. They are a practical way of living based on a magical mind-set. Many of them, those that are important to life, have passed over into the cult and been shaped by it. But cult in a religious sense exists only where there is real religion. Perhaps people can both work and serve their fields and grain with magic, with rites that create and increase power. But these rites become religion and cult only when they are related to the holy and when power is experienced as holy power or a gift from the holy—in other words, when and if these actions are regarded as a response to a call from holy powers, from the holy. Cult, then, is derived from religion.[6] In essence, religion and magic are different. In magic, people are dealing with more or less impersonal, undifferentiated powers that the skilled person can master according to known laws with powerful, efficacious means, exercising practices that compel these powers to act. In religion, one has to deal with a personal power on whom one is completely dependent and whom one approaches with fear and trembling because that power is different from oneself and transcends human calculations, abilities, and will.

It is this very essence of religion that meets us at the foundation of Israel's cult. It is true, as we have said, that the forms of cult necessarily have taken over many elements from the magical view of reality—rites, actions, and words—that originally developed from the primitive mind's rational use of regular if nonetheless mysterious means to make the power useful for the creation and advancement of life. But these elements have been drawn into the sphere of religion, become part of the cult, part of the social manifestation of the relationship between the religious

---

6. Cf. Underhill, *Worship*; and Will, *Le Culte*; also Quell, *Das kultische Problem der Psalmen*, 35ff.

community and a personal, divine power who does that which it will and whom humans must serve in order to win its goodwill and who creates and gives of its own freewill. In such a cult, the originally magical elements are redefined and changed into an expression of something quite different from what they may have originally meant, changed into expressions of a relationship to the deity and for the deity's actions with the religious community and the world of the religious community. Of course, this does not exclude the possibility of the magical element as described above taking over the religious element in the cult—at least in certain respects. Moreover, the "primitive" thoughts can stubbornly survive and occasionally re-emerge. This also occurred in Israel's cult. But to a great extent, in Israel's cult we are dealing with a serving and receiving mutual relationship between the religious community and a God who acts and gives freely.

5 | Holiness and the Holy One

PIETY

Many books have been written about what the essence of religion really is. Religion is said to have arisen from fear. It is said to be a sublimation or an absolutizing of paternal authority or of the relationship to father and mother. Religion's essence is said to be a transcendental tendency on the part of humans. Perhaps better defined, religion is the complete response of humanity to a compelling call that comes to it. But perhaps one comes even closer to the heart of the matter if one says that the encounter with the powerful becomes religion when it shapes a relationship that is permeated with "piety." Piety is not only a feeling that accompanies something else; rather, it is an active, spiritual, total commitment to something uplifted that one experiences as real and to which one considers oneself to be dependent upon and with whom one sees oneself as standing in a mutual relationship. The ancient Latin expression for this was *pietas*, a dutiful obligation of respect and affection for all of the real factors and relationships that a person was set in—the relationship to God, to one's elders, to one's family, to the state, to work, and so forth.

SACRED AND PROFANE

The way to clarity about this matter, it seems to me, has been the direction laid out by such scholars as Nathan Söderblom and Rudolf Otto, with their emphasis on the sacred. Piety has always been certain that it stood over against something that was "sacred."

Religious experience and religious relationship are tied to an experience of the sacred. Religion occurs when humans experience a meeting with that sacred. A certainty about this is a fundamental element of all religion.[1] It involves not merely power or powers but *sacred* power. "That person is pious for whom something is holy" (Söderblom).

The certitude about something holy cannot be derived from any speculation or reflection but must be based on experience, a perception of something that declares itself to humanity's certainty as separate from the ordinary, as different from all else and at the same time more real and more powerful than all else. Separated from the ordinary—the profane—is in many languages the basic meaning of the word that corresponds to that which we call "holy." So are both the Latin word *sanctus* (from *sancire* = to separate) and the Hebrew word *qadosh*.

The word "holy/sacred" covers a broad spectrum, including experience, feeling, and intellect. Still, the basic elements are the same in all religions and languages. One can try to determine its content psychologically by taking account of the most powerful feelings the sacred releases or in terms of comparative religion and phenomenology by analyzing the properties involved.

Humanity stands trembling before the sacred. "Fear of God" in the Old Testament is the expression for that which we call religion. It does not mean primarily fear in the sense of anxiety, but rather of respect and awe. Humanity meets the sacred with humility. One becomes convinced of one's lowliness. One feels the distance. "Woe is me, I am lost," says Isaiah (Isa 6:5). "Go away from me, Lord," Peter bursts out (Luke 5:8). But humans also feel mysteriously attracted. One feels "uplifted," "enraptured," and

---

1. See Acts 17. Cf. Söderblom, *Gudstrons Uppkomst*, 198ff., and s.v. "Helig" and "Helighet"; Lehmann, *Religionens Välrld*, 55ff.; R. Otto, *Das Heilige* [ET: *The Idea of the Holy*]; van der Leeuw, *Phänomenologie*, 8ff., and s.v. "Heilig" and "Heillgkeit" [ET: *Religion in Essence and Manifestation*, 28, and s.v. "Holiness, holy"]; Widengren, *Religionens Värld*, 28–77; Pedersen, *Israel*, III–IV:12–15, and s.v. "Holiness."

"carried away."[2] This bifurcation, this tension between two poles, exultation and fear, is utterly characteristic of religion, the relationship to the sacred.[3]

The sacred is that which is "totally other" than any other thing. It is different from and, for that matter, opposed to the "every day," the "profane" (Hebrew *chol*). The sacred is elevated, fearful, and completely awe-inspiring, as is humanity's perception of it. The sacred sets itself at a distance and attracts to itself. It humbles and it uplifts.

SACRALITY AND POWER, FETISHES

But above all, the sacred is powerful—that is, full of power. Those concepts—*mana* and the sacred—are therefore so closely related that the same word contains both aspects. Power always has something of holiness about it. Hence, it is fully understandable that humanity, probably from the very beginning, found the sacred to be wherever there is power. And power stirs up fear, reverence, wonder, and attraction. It is important to approach it with the right relationship. One of the first stages, then, along the development of religion is to find, gather, arrange, and preserve those things that are full of power and to treat them correctly in order to use them for good fortune, progress, or "salvation." This is how such sacred objects arose that we call fetishes, such as the *nkisi* bags of the tribes in the Congo and many similar things.[4] Something of the same idea is involved in superstitions concerning amulets, relics of saints, talismans, or mascots. When such fetishes are venerated with anointing or sacrifices that bring power and regarded as the abode of more or less personal beings, they have become sacred and divine and can be "gods." It comes to expression when such a "manufactured object"—the actual

---

2. Cf. Berggrav, *Den Religiøse Følelse i Sundt Sjeleliv*, 97ff.
3. Cf. Bertholet, "Religionsgeschichtliche Ambivalenzerscheinungen."
4. See Briem, *På Trons Tröskel*, 55ff.; van der Leeuw, *Phänomenologie*, 17ff., 427ff. [ET: *Religion in Essence and Manifestation*, 37–40, 449–53].

meaning of the Portuguese word *feiticio*—is made more or less in human form.

When in the Old Testament the sacred and "the Holy One of Israel" are mentioned, in general there is a notion of both power and a miraculous power that is capable of creating, blessing, protecting, or destroying. The Holy One of Israel is a fortress and a source of power for his people, but he is a destructive terror for his enemies. "Power" and "powers" have generally been perceived in the history of religion as sacred, separated, surrounded with all kinds of precautions and tabus. Yahweh's holy ark is a protection for his people in battle, but there also proceeds from it a dangerous power that kills whoever gets involved with it in an inappropriate fashion or without respecting the proper rules. So we hear about Uzzah when David brought the ark up to Jerusalem. With the best of intentions, he reached out with his hand and touched the ark at the point of its falling from the cart, but "The anger of Yahweh was kindled against Uzzah; and God struck him there because he reached out his hand to the ark; and he died there beside the ark of God" (2 Sam 6:6–7; see 1 Sam 6:1—7:2).[5] Before the sacred, humans live in a tension between apparently conflicting feelings and reactions.

Different religions emphasize various aspects of these contradictory sides of the sacred. The Persians and the Arctic tribes experienced the sacred especially in the vital forces of creation, fertility, and health. They saw the interrelationship of "whole," "holy," and prosperity. The Semites—and above all the Old Testament—emphasized the distance of the deities, their awesome power and otherness. They perceived them as majestic by reason of its awesome power and distance. They stir up fear and trembling by reason of their majesty and are seen also as both creating and dangerously destructive. Compared to holiness or to the Holy One, humans are lowly, weak, and "unclean."

---

5. [Ed.] Mowinckel cites only 1 Sam 6:19–20, while the broader context is necessary.

Holiness and the Holy One

The power and quality of the sacred is transmitted—and this is the genuinely primitive thought—to everything that has anything to do with it and thus make them holy: places, times, persons, rites, words, implements, etc. (2 Sam 6:6-15; cf. Hag 2:12-14.). From the primitive viewpoint, holiness in the ancient religions shares in all the properties of power. The holy must also be surrounded with all kinds of rules of holiness similar to the old tabu rules. It must be approached in the right way by the right persons according to the right procedures. Holy and tabu often become the same thing just as power and holiness. In the Polynesian languages, the concept of tabu most often means quite simply holiness,[6] just as the Hebrew word for holy, *qadosh*, sometimes indicates simply what we mean by tabu: forbidden and dangerous. The holy can also bring both prosperity and death.[7] But it is supreme to a totally different degree than anything else. It sets its own rules and cannot be compelled by anyone. It is divine and yet on the other hand in the Old Testament the entire essence of the deity can be simply expressed with the word 'holy': "I Yahweh your God am holy" (e.g., Lev 19:2); Yahweh is "the Holy One of Israel" (e.g., Isa 1:4).

In the term 'holy' is consequently expressed the experience of the powers as something numinous, the "divinization" of the powers.

THE HOLY ONE, GODS

"Divinization" is a natural result of the "magical-mythical" thinking—not to mention the metaphysical background—including the construction of power, or in other words: the acquisition of power. We have already seen that the distinction between personal and impersonal is actually not characteristic of primitive peoples. We find everywhere a smooth transition from the idea of power the same as an "impersonal" imagined power substance

---

6. See Briem, *På Trons Tröskel*, 62ff.
7. See n. 5 above.

or power flow, as with the blood or the breath of life, the idea of personal liability, although still highly undifferentiated "powers." And power—especially power as consciously experienced and perceived the sacred—has a pronounced tendency to become a power system.

To express it in mythological language, everything that is experienced as particularly powerful forces—both positively and negatively—that are of crucial importance for life, enter into the sphere of religion and become holy, numinous, "divine" essence. The sacred powers then are experienced as sacred essence, as gods.

Religion deals not only with the concept of the sacred, then, but proceeds immediately over to the concept of the Holy One. Holiness is something that belongs to the Holy One and the holy ones and can be mediated from them to other beings, places, objects, or actions. God is the sacred power. The words for "God" may have different etymologies, as is often pointed out. The Norse *god*—tellingly originally a neuter—actually means "the one called upon," "the one summoned." The basic meaning of the Semitic word for God (*ilu*, *'el*, etc.) is 'power.' The same is the case with the Egyptian word *neter* with the meaning of deity or divinity. Holiness indicates in the Old Testament for all practical purposes the same thing as divinity. The "holy ones" means also the divine beings (the sons of God) who exist alongside Yahweh. And he is himself the Holy One, the Holy One of Israel, pure and simple.

As far as power was concerned, it was an easy and fluid transition from the concept of an impersonal, materially perceived quality to the concept of personal if nevertheless highly undifferentiated set of powers. In that sense, one can speak of gods which have resulted from power, or "*mana* gods." The holy and the divine were seen directly in the powerful. The powerful becomes the divine. Power can be perceived as a god. We see this, for example, in the American Indian tribes where Wakanda or Manitu—their words for power or the powerful one—were partly perceived as a more or less personal divine essence, a kind of highest god working in everything. Perhaps such a god is not worshipped with any kind of cult in the real sense. But he is experienced as existing through the strong feelings that accompany efficacious ritual acts and which are a proof that the worshippers themselves have been filled with Wakanda.[8] The sacred has all of the qualities that make it into something personal. But let us be clear that this distinction, which is a sharp one for us, was not so clear for the primitive mind. For people of ancient times, it was normal, as we have seen, to perceive animals, things, places, powers, and properties as part of that which we would call personal realities or beings. We see this also in the religion of Old Testament. It was very easy to think of God's properties, Yahweh's "judgment," his "arm," his "spirit," and so forth as something more or less personal and independent, i.e., as hypostases.[9]

GODS, ANCESTORS, AND THE SACRAL KING

The perception and the experience of the holy or the Holy One draws spontaneously to itself and, therefore, into the religious sphere all of those things and essences which are experienced as powerful and desirable. Persons, animals, and things are full of *mana* and can become gods, as we saw. Divinity reveals itself in those powerful essences that promote life. In grain, it is the grain god such as the Semitic Dagan, who shows himself, grows, dies, gives nourishment, and is resurrected to a new life. In the fertility of nature, the god is active. He or she is revealed in the life of nature and gives, through the rites of the cult, a share in his or her power. Such gods are the Semitic fertility gods such as Tammuz, Ba'al or "the Lord"—"the uplifted Lord of the earth"—Adonis, the mother goddess Astarte, or the virgin Anat, Ishtar of the Babylonians, and many others.

---

8. Briem, *På Trons Tröskel*, 43ff., 48ff., 59ff.
9. Cf. Mowinckel, "Hypostasen"; see also Pss 43:3; 44:4; 89:3 (conjecture).

Moreover, those powers that undergird the community as justice, truth, the law of life, and so forth can be seen as divine powers. The Semites' Misharu (justice), Kettu (truth), Shalem (peace), Ṣedeq (the purveyor of judgment), the Egyptian's Ma'at (truth or law), and the Persian Amesha Spentas became such cosmic-social gods.

The totem ancestors and the benevolent and protective totem essences embodied in animals or plants can also become deities, and the ceremonies that seek to increase power and prosperity of the totem animal or plant can become a cult. Totemism thereby receives a more or less religious element.[10]

Among the "mighty ones" are the dead ancestors who from the very beginning have been drawn into the sphere of the holy and into the world of religion. They include not just anybody who is dead, but the dead patriarch, chief, founder, the mythical pioneers, or the medicine men, for example. They live on not only in the grave or in the distant world, but also by incorporating themselves partly into their descendants and partly in holy things, places, and people. The community maintains the relationship with them in order to share in their power so that the dead can protect their clan and their people and give them power, fertility, and life. Ancestor veneration is among the most widespread phenomena in the world of religion.[11] It was fundamental to the religion of the ancient Semites. Holiness and power were especially present at the graves of the fathers. This was true even in most ancient Israel (viz. before Moses). Traces of it can

---

10. Briem's criticism of the view of totemism as a religious phenomenon (*På Trons Tröskel*, 278) is justified, but it goes too far. The material he presents shows that the totem essences are perceived as helpers and as powerful or holy and are received with honor, and have their worship in the form of ceremonies of intimacy that increase power. These are not purely magical in the sense of profane. See Grønbech in *Illustreret Religionshistorie*, 63ff.

11. See van der Leeuw, *Phänomenologie*, 111ff. [ET: *Religion in Essence and Manifestation*, 130–31]; Birkeli, *Religionshistorie*, 1:106ff. and below, p. 69 n. 42.

be found in the Old Testament.[12] It lives again in much of the veneration of saints' graves in Palestine, in Christianity as well as in Judaism and Islam.

But also living persons can have such power and holiness that they become objects of veneration. If the father of a clan lives on in the chieftain or king, then he shares in the divinity of the clan father. All of the community's holiness is concentrated in him; he becomes the source of blessing and power for the people and creates rain and fertility and prosperity for them and as such is surrounded by all of the tabu rules of holiness. We find this among the Polynesian and African kings and the emperor in Japan. And from these rainmaker kings, as they have been called, who are one with the father of the clan, there goes a line back to the divine pharaoh of Egypt," "the good god" who is one with the dead Osiris and the reborn Horus and unites in himself both life and death, both Horus and Seth, the two powers in the cycle of life. From life till death and from death till life. The sacred king is also one of religion's holy powers. We find this concept of the king as more or less divine also in the other religions of the ancient Near East—among the Sumerians, the Babylonians, and the Hittites. Also in ancient Israel, the king was regarded as holy and as the son of Yahweh endowed with the spirit of Yahweh through anointing, and he is an *'elohim*, a divine essence, a channel for the blessing of the deity. But expressly Yahwism made the son relationship of the king into an adoptive relationship and emphasized increasingly his representing the people before Yahweh instead of representing Yahweh before the people.[13]

---

12. See Pedersen, *Israel*, III–IV:213, 479–86.

13. Concerning sacral kingship, see Frankfort, *Kingship and the Gods*; Engnell, *Studies in Divine Kingship*; Widengren, *Religionens Värld*, 248ff., which to some extent exaggerates the matter. For the divinity of the king in Israel, see especially Gunkel, *Einleitung in die Psalmen*, 155ff. [ET: *Introduction to Psalms*, 109–13]; Mowinckel, *Kongesalmerne*, 20ff.

PERSONAL AND IMPERSONAL

"Folk psychology" has tried to explain how the concept of personal gods arose by pointing out the tendency to personify the holy. But one could also point out the natural tendency to conceive of the active realities of life in human terms, as thinking, feeling, willing, and acting beings. Or one could point out the intellectual need to find an author of existence and assume that this need has united itself with the experience of the holy and has given the deity a personal character. All these are artificial constructions and, in fact, explain little. For religion itself and its thought—theology—the matter is much simpler. The distinction between personal and impersonal, as we explain it when we survey the history of religion, is less important than we might believe, because for the early stages we are now discussing it is really an artificial distinction. The ancients always regarded everything that was alive as more or less personal or connected it with something personal. There was not an "evolution" from a stage when powers were regarded as "impersonal" to a "higher" stage with "personal" powers. The holy immediately becomes the holy ones, so to speak. In the religious experience and act, man's "I" is silent before a "Thou," which he sees without reflection in a certain analogy with himself. We shall come back to this in the chapter about the origin of religion.

POLYTHEISM, HENOTHEISM, MONOTHEISM, AND PANTHEISM

There are thus "many gods and many lords," as Paul writes (1 Cor 8:5). But polytheism is really not characteristic of religion, even of the "pagan" religions. In any, case, it is incorrect to draw an overarching line of development from polydaimonism to polytheism and then to monotheism. In religious experience itself and, therefore, in cult, humanity is dealing with the One. That which is of significance for humanity is not whether there are one or many, but that the one they are dealing with is the *only* one.[14] The question is whether or not they have approached the incomparable, the unique, who is so considered and who is certainly bigger, more powerful, and different than all the others.[15] Therefore, there is no original element in religion that says that gods are specialists—that there is a god for this or that activity or this or that phenomenon of nature. A real god is simply god, the god who stands for all of the needs and blessings of the worshipping person or community and everything that the community or person lives on. "Nature worship" is really a misleading expression. If a god, for example, is understood as the sun god or the rain god or such, it is not only the sun or the rain that in and of itself is worshipped, but that god whose power expresses itself in the sun or the rain is also the god of all of the goods and values of life upon which the worshipping community is dependent. Warmth and rain are among the most important, but the god's power and jurisdiction is not limited by them. It is not the grain that one worships but the grain god, and he has to do with more than only the grain. The Canaanite Dagan or Dagon became both a city god and a war god. The fertility goddess, Anat, who battled for Ba'al against Mot (Death), was also a goddess of war, and as such, the Egyptians came to recognize this particular Canaanite deity. When the clan whom Abraham represents worshipped the god of Abraham,[16] it occurred because Abraham and his people had found that he was the god for them.

It is a question here not of any theoretical monotheism but of a more or less exclusive relationship to the power that manifests itself to the worshipper as God—or, if one wishes, to whose form God has revealed himself to the worshipper. This has been called henotheism. Such an exclusivity can become conscious and obligatory. This is what happened in Israel. "Yahweh is a jealous god," who will not share his honor with any other. There

---

14. Cf. Johnson, *The One and the Many*.

15. Cf. van der Leeuw, *Phänomenologie*, 164ff. [ET: *Religion in Essence and Manifestation*, 182–87].

16. Cf. Alt, "Der Gott der Väter" [ET: "The God of the Fathers"].

came early to the leading circles a conviction that the covenant between Yahweh and Israel, the choice of this people "that Yahweh should be their god and they his people" also meant that he alone could demand to be worshipped on the part of the people. Monolatry, the worship of one god, is what this practical and conscious exclusivity has been called.

Polytheism with a well-ordered hierarchy of the gods, each of whom ruled his special area of existence, and with a supreme god, a father god, or a divine king at the pinnacle is the result of a long political and theological process. In a large state, worship of the gods of many landscapes and tribes was subordinated to the god of the ruling clan, class, or city. Theological thought ordered these in an hierarchical system that set off the different areas of power one from the other working out the specialization of the gods. One had the authority to deal with the sun, another had to deal with the moon, a third with thunder and rain, a fourth with justice, a fifth with oracles, and so forth.

Monotheism can be the result of an exclusive monolatry, as in Israel. The other gods are reduced to subordinated servants, angels, demons, or even powerless non-entities. There is only one Lord and God. Yahweh will not share his supremacy with anyone whether in the cult of Israel or in the government of the world. Everything is in his hand, and he created it. He is all-powerful over people, kingdoms, nature, history, and the destiny of individual men. He also demands supremacy over hearts, wills, and feelings. "You shall love Yahweh your God with all your heart, and with all your soul, and with all your might" (Deut 6:5). The intellectual process comes to this notion and shapes it and justifies it, but it did not create it. Yahweh is no abstract philosophical deity but an all powerful lord.

But monotheism can also begin as a philosophical idea about a single god as the summation of the laws, principles, and powers of existence. Monotheism was of this philosophical sort in Greek thought and Indian speculation. Monotheism of this kind can easily become a more or less vague pantheism. God is the principal of life in everything that is, or the world soul, or an apotheosis of the law of nature, and the like. Mysticism (see below) is often part of this philosophical, comprehensive deity, but it gives the notion a warm, personal tone through the mystical experience of being absorbed in the "Unity."

DIVINITY, THE SOURCE OF HOLINESS

For us as we try to make a kind of overview by setting off boundaries and systematizing, it can seem that the concept of God arose from the concept of holiness, that the god is born of holiness. This is incorrect because that is an external view of the situation. For religion itself, it is clear that the certainty about standing vis-à-vis something "different," something holy occurs where divinity is experienced, where the deity confronts humanity and makes himself known. The certainty of holiness is the soul's reaction to something that is experienced. "Something" meets humanity and calls forth in one's soul certain reactions which take a definite form in the conviction that what one is meeting is "holy." It is this psychological side of the experience that Rudolph Otto has tried to analyze. What he has found encompasses two opposing feelings: fear and attraction. The holy or the Holy One are simultaneously that which awakens fear and that which draws to itself: *mysterium tremendum et fascinans*. This notion is expressed well in the narrative about Moses and the burning bush. Yahweh shows himself in the real flames that nonetheless do not burn the bush (Exod 3:2). Moses wants to come closer and see this "miracle." Then comes the word (the proclamation): "Remove the sandals from your feet, for the place on which you are standing is holy ground" (3:5b) Moses reacts with a feeling of certainty about the holy, and this reaction of certainty includes both fear and reverence: "Come no closer!" (3:5a) and the attracting notion that he will nonetheless approach the flames. The certainty about holiness is derived from the experience of the deity.

For religious thought, this means that the deity is the origin and the source of holiness. A thing, a place, a person, and so forth can be holy because it belongs to the deity.

In the Old Testament, it is completely clear that it is the Holy One, not indefinite holy powers that the people are dealing with in the cult. Yahweh is "the Holy One," "the Holy One of Israel," "the holy God who does not die," the threefold holy that Isaiah experiences in connection with the cultic feast. All holiness stems from Yahweh. All holiness—things, places, times, persons, actions in the cult—derive their holiness from him. They are holy because they belong to him and are arranged and ordered by him. True, we encounter some remnants of older concepts about places, springs, trees, stones, and so forth which have holy power themselves. But even they are increasingly led back to their establishment by Yahweh.

Holiness makes demands on anyone who deals with it. Because it is other, humans must act differently and be different. Whoever wishes to approach the holy must "sanctify himself."[17] This is not limited to humanity's participation in the time of the cult. Holiness is disseminated to all who deal with it. In the Old Testament a demand is made on the entire community, the entire people, that they must constantly be holy because they are the people of the Holy One. "You shall be holy for I, Yahweh, your God am holy."[18] This became a demand for permanent quality in a determined way of life and morality.

SYMBOLS

In worship, human beings have to deal with the holy and the Holy One, with divinity. There they encounter him, worship him, and serve him. Cult is proximity to the deity and indeed contact with divinity. The deity comes and is sought out and encountered in certain places and at certain times (see below), and he is near

---

17. Cf. Exod 19:10–15; 1 Sam 21:5–6.

18. See also: Lev 18:4–6, 30; 19:2–3, 10, 12, 14, 16, 18, 25, 27, 29, 31–32, 34, 36–37; 20:7, 24, 26; 21:6, 15, etc.

wherever cult takes place. The nearness of the deity is experienced in the soul, in the strong and moving feelings that stream through it and often lift it above itself in ecstasy. But it is also present in the inner yielding of trust and belief.

But there is an universal psychological need to have perceptible testimonies of the nearness of the deity, guarantees that make it realistic and beyond dispute. For this reason, symbols have their place in the cult.[19] The deity's reality and proximity are symbolized by something perceptible that at the same time "represents" the deity and shares in his essence and strength and mediates it further to the community.

Such symbols can be of many kinds, such as the holy stone or rock; the formless fetish; the posts, the doorposts, or the balcony inside the house; the depiction in animal or human form; or symbolic ideograms, such as the cross and the elements of the Lord's Supper. An image in animal or human form represents an advanced cultural stage; neither the ancient Arabs[20] nor the tribes of Israel had any actual images of the gods.[21]

But something in the very essence of religion resists clear, rational pictures of the divine. The one who is completely different cannot be represented in any realistic form. Therefore, the cultic picture is often regarded as degenerate, and in religion there can often be serious argument about the image of a god.

The religion of Israel also had its symbols for God. Such was Yahweh's holy box—"the ark"[22]—or the oracular case with the two holy oracular devices, the Urim and Thummim.[23] All such symbols were thought to be filled with something of the deity's own holiness and power. They were holy and had their

---

19. Cf. Underhill, *Worship*, 37ff.

20. See Wellhausen, *Reste arabischen Heidentums*, 102.

21. Cf. Hvidberg, *Den israelistiske Religions Historie*, 76; Mowinckel, *Le Decalogue*, 71.

22. Cf. Mowinckel in *GTMMM*, vol. 2: *De tidligere profeter*; note 1 Sam 14:37a.

23. Ibid., see 1 Sam 14:3c and 37a.

own tabu rules. Thus, there is in the consciousness of the believers no sharp distinction between fetishes and the cultic symbols of the deity. In other words, fetishes, relics, and so forth are an expression of the need to have the deity near in some perceptible symbol. One example is Israel's concept of Yahweh's sacred ark. Wherever it was, Yahweh himself was present, efficacious, and powerful. But it was also thought of in such a way that the divine power of itself was present, working for the blessing and victory for Israel and the defeat of its enemies. To lay a hand on the ark without heeding the ritual regulations brought death immediately upon the one who approached it, as we hear of David's servant, Uzza. Nonetheless, the ark stood in a house of Obed-edom and brought blessing over him and all that belonged to him. Under the influence of Canaanite culture, there came, for a time, images of the deity even into the cult of Yahweh. Yahweh was even depicted in the form of a bull in certain holiness rituals. But for those who maintained the traditions of the Mosaic era, this was regarded as something strange and wrong.[24] Less than anyone else could Yahweh be depicted in any visible form. His symbol became the empty throne of the cherubs,[25] where he could be thought to reign invisibly, and the box (the ark) became his hassock;[26] but to some extent, it shared in the power of his holiness.[27] He himself was hidden, but the watchful eye could occasionally perceive his majesty, the radiance that surrounded him.[28] The writer of the epic did not mean that the box was in itself magical, for it was "God who struck Uzzah" and who "blessed the house of Obed-edom."[29]

---

24. Hvidberg, *Den israelistiske Religions Historie*, pp. 75ff.; Mowinckel, *Le Decalogue*, 71ff.; Mowinckel, "A quelle moment le culte de Jahve."

25. Cf. H. Schmidt, "Keruben-Thron und Lade"; Pedersen, *Israel*, III–IV:229–34.

26. Ps 132:7.

27. Cf. Hvidberg, *Den israelistiske Religions Historie*, 176ff.

28. Cf. *GTMMM*, 1:137–38, on Exod 16:7a.

29. 2 Sam 6:6ff., 11.

6 | Fellowship
God and Community

THE COMMUNITY, THE CULTIC ASSEMBLY

The cult is not primarily a private affair, but rather a matter of fellowship. Behind every cult there always stands a community as its earthly subject.[1]

The oldest form of human life is a common life. It was also true in ancient Israel that the given reality, the unity, in human life dealt not with the life of individuals but with fellowship, the group: the family, clan, tribe, city, and nation.[2] Moreover, in Christian worship even today the truth that lies in this perception is experienced anew: that the congregation at worship is a fellowship. There is something essential about religion that it creates community and emerges as a fellowship and as a unit. Seen from this viewpoint, the most powerful expression of the essence of worship and its content are given in Jesus' words: "For where two or three are gathered in my name, I am there among them" (Matt 18:20). Here are given both fellowship among members of the assembly (even if it numbers only two or three) and fellowship with the Lord whom they have gathered to meet and who comes and emerges in the assembly with them and shares their intention. "In my name," that is to say, in order to serve him or to be one with him spiritually "conformed to the image of his [God's] son," as Paul expresses it (Rom 8:29). It is expressed again when this mutual fellowship between

---

1. Cf. Strom, *Religion och Gemenskap*; and van der Leeuw, *Phänomenologie*, 223ff. [ET: *Religion in Essence and Manifestation*, 242–74].

2. Cf. Pedersen, *Israel*, I–II:29–60, 263–78; Robinson, "The Hebrew Conception of Corporate Personality."

brothers is deepened and realized in action. Worship is the fellowship's meeting for fellowship with divinity, with the Lord, in order to receive something that all can give to and receive from one another. The Israelites' word for this religious fellowship was "covenant" (*berith*). The people of the covenant appear in the cult as the "assembly" (*qahal, 'eda*).[3]

Fellowship can be of many kinds. It can be the natural units: family, clan, tribe, people.[4] But there can also be a smaller group within the unit that usually has a more or less closed, esoteric stamp of its own with rites and procedures that are kept secret.[5] Often the cultic community is the men's community or the assembly of adult males where boys are taken in at the age of puberty. There can also be secret societies of men with their own rites and specific intentions that can develop, for example, into political or terrorist cabals. One special type of such extraordinary cultic assemblies is the sect.[6]

But the cultic assembly can also be broadened to include an association of clans and tribes that for one or more reasons are closely related to one another. For example, they have the same language or dwelling place. The Greek amphictyonies were such cultic groups: unions of tribes with both religious and political goals, but whose first task was maintaining the common worship of that deity who was the special god of the association. An example would be Apollo in Delphi and his oracle. But fellowship can also go beyond the more narrow foundation given by nature in family and country and find its core in fellowship around a deity and so become a supranational "church."[7]

---

3. Cf. Rost, *Die Vorstufen von Kirche und Synagoge im Alten Testament*, 7ff., 38ff.

4. Cf. van der Leeuw, *Phänomenologie*, 225ff. [ET: *Religion in Essence and Manifestation*, 245–51.].

5. Ibid., 232ff.; Birket-Smith, *Kulturens Veje*, 2:52ff. [ET: *Paths of Culture*.]

6. Cf. van der Leeuw, *Phänomenologie*, 242ff. [ET: *Religion in Essence and Manifestation*, 261–64.].

7. Ibid., 245ff. [ET: 265–68].

Fellowship

In Israel, we have clear traces of these properties in the cultic assembly. "The assembly of Israel" meant both Israel gathered for common worship and the summoning of Israel's men for common military or political action.[8] It was composed originally of the adult males. Only with the beginning of their thirteenth year could boys be admitted to the assembly,[9] and circumcision, which later was undertaken when boys were eight days of age, was originally a cultic action and a rite of passage for sexually mature boys.[10] In Judaism, the full obligation to keep the law began only at the end of the twelfth year.[11] And even today in [orthodox] Jewish synagogues, women have their own place behind a screen in the gallery.[12] They are an adjunct to the cultic assembly.

We also find clear traces of the community of union in Israel. The people in Israel became a "covenant community" composed of many tribes around the worship of the covenant god (Ba'al berit).[13] This was Yahweh of Kadesh-Sinai, and in the earliest years after settling in Palestine—the time of the judges—Israel comprised an amphictyony[14] of ten tribes.[15] Their first common

---

8. Cf. Rost, *Die Vorstufen von Kirche und Synagoge im Alten Testament*, summarized on 31ff., 75–76.

9. Cf. Ezra 3:64 in the Greek text of so-called 3 Ezra.

10. There is a trace of this in Exod 4:24–26.

11. See Schürer, *Geschichte des jüdischen Volkes im Zeitalter Jesu Christi*, II:492ff. [ET: *The History of the Jewish People in the Time of Jesus Christ*].

12. See Elbogen, *Der jüdischen Gottesdienst*, 423, 435–36, 466ff.

13. Judg 9:4, 46.

14. See Noth, *Das System der zwölf Stämme Israels*.

15. This appears, among other places, in the enumeration of the twelve tribes in the ancient poetry of Judges 5. The twelve-tribe schema first shows up with the kingdom of David, which united Judah with Israel. It has always been an artificial schema. "Levi" was never a real tribe, but indicated the priestly class; Simeon no longer existed at that time, and Joseph was counted sometimes as one tribe and sometimes as two (Ephraim and Manasseh) and sometimes, oddly, as three (Joseph, Ephraim, and Manasseh). This is so in Deut 5:33, tribal poetry which probably stemmed from the Northern Kingdom in the period after the division of the Kingdom around 932 BCE (see *GTMMM*, I:421–22).

task was to maintain public national worship of Yahweh and support one another in war. They took part in common punishment against such tribes or groups who were guilty of breaking the duties of the covenant or holy tradition.[16] Among the Jews we also find hints of the creation of a "congregation" that extended beyond blood relationship[17] and could admit non-Israelites as proselytes.[18]

Since worship is an exercise of fellowship in mutual giving and sharing and of common "power," the action of being received into the cult and the rites of passage are so important.[19] They consist of both efficacious symbols and rites for increasing power—which in time can degenerate into sadistic torture and "manhood tests" as among the old Spartans and many Indian tribes—and in the mediation of the society's more or less secret traditions, first and foremost those about cultic rights and their meaning and effect.[20] One such rite of passage was, as we have said, the circumcision ritual of the Israelites. Another was Christian baptism, which had its forerunners in similar ceremonies in late Jewish circles. It means being received and incorporated into the fellowship. Behind these actions stands the deity himself, and these actions came about because he began them. Circumcision was the "sign of the covenant" that Yahweh had ordained. Christian baptism is reception as part of "the body of Christ" and leads one into the life and death community with Christ himself. It gives a share both in his death and in "the power of his resurrection."[21]

16. This is the ancient core of the strongly reworked tradition in Judges 19–21.

17. Cf. Rost, *Die Vorstufen von Kirche und Synagoge im Alten Testament*.

18. Cf. Schürer, *Geschichte des jüdischen Volkes im Zeitalter Jesu Christi*, III:150ff. [ET: *The History of the Jewish People in the Time of Jesus Christ*].

19. Cf. van der Leeuw, *Phänomenologie*, 177ff., 506ff. [ET: *Religion in Essence and Manifestation*, 192–205, 529–34].

20. So, for example, among the Australian Aborigines. Cf. Söderblom, *Gudstons Uppkomst*, 141. 152, 182; cf. 144–45. Birket Smith, *Kulturens Veje*, 2:100ff. [ET: *Paths of Culture*].

21. Cf. Brun, *Paulus' Kristelige Tanker*, 126ff., 174ff., 182ff.

Fellowship

In the Masonic lodges of recent times with their mixed religious and social stamp, rites of initiation play the greatest role. The actual sum and substance of the lodges' life is experienced in them. These ceremonies provide the most important opportunities for the members to meet.

Another aspect of worship's social character is the element of exclusivity that permeates it. The cult is not for outsiders. The whole family[22] or all the adult males meet,[23] but the others—or, in a later stage, certain classes of persons—are excluded.[24] The older cults often have the character of mysteries, closed communities where one is received through rites of initiation that are kept secret from everyone else.[25] Later, worship became something for the whole family, tribe, or nation, or for the members, i.e., the believers. Even in early Christianity, the unbaptized had to leave when one came to the high point of worship, the Lord's Supper.

There are, to be sure, some cultic activities that exist for the sake of the individual. But they exist only because he is a member of a community, and the community stands behind him with the solidity of its "wholeness."

FELLOWSHIP WITH THE DEITY

But in worship, there is something higher. The community seeks fellowship with the deity. If one looks at it from the outside, it often seems as though worship is something that proceeds from the people. In a sense, this does happen. Humans "seek God." But the community knows that it is not trying to find something it invented. God has made himself known to it and made it seek

---

22. Cf. 1 Sam 20:5–6, 26–27, 28–29.

23. See Exod 23:17; 34:23; Deut 16:16.

24. Deut 23:1–3; 2 Sam 5:8b. Cf. the many *leges sacrae* (sacral laws) from various "judgments of holiness" which determine who may not have access to the sacred place, or establish the conditions of access. Cf. Mowinckel, *Le Decalogue*, 147ff.; or see Psalms 15 and 24:3–6; Mic 6:6–8; Isa 33:14–16.

25. Cf. Nilsson, *Primitive Religion*, 96ff.; Söderblom, *Ur Religionens Historia*, 99–100.

him. Even in the most primitive worship, such as that of the Aborigines in Australia, the "congregation" is convinced that it is dealing with things that have been given to it, taught and revealed at the dawn of time by the great "original beings."[26] In Israel's religion, the expression "seek God" was a cultic expression from the very beginning and meant to seek and receive an oracle or other help from the deity in the holy place and in union with sacred rites; but the idea of God's initiative comes completely to the fore. God "reveals himself" or "shows himself to" the patriarchs, and wherever this happened, they built an altar and worshipped. God teaches Moses how to seek and worship him on behalf of the people—the community. He points out the holy cultic places and promises to come to them and give his blessing.[27] God "lets himself to be found," and he "finds" and "grasps." In the cultic festival, "God makes himself known." Through Moses, Yahweh has commanded the whole cultic life, that through it people shall be renewed and be able to uphold their "covenant" with him.[28]

Still, the boundary between the initiative of God and the community is fluid. Worship is a relationship of mutual interaction between God and the community but of a sort that the usual words "subject" and "object" have only relative validity—as in religion generally. Humanity seeks and is sought, finds and is found, gives—in sacrifice and gifts—but only of that which it has received. It receives in order to have something to give.

Holiness proceeds from Yahweh and his holiness to everything and everyone involved in the worship of him. The community must "sanctify itself" through certain cleansing processes and temperance, and it must leave behind its normal profane condition in order to take part in worship and to enter the sphere

---

26. Cf. Söderblom, *Gudstrons Uppkommst*, 123–24.

27. Exod 20:24.

28. This side of religion's own perception of worship is rightly emphasized by Quell, *Das kultische Problem der Psalmen*, 47; cf. van der Leeuw, *Phänomenologie*, 3, 317 [ET: *Religion in Essence and Manifestation*].

Fellowship

of the sacred.[29] All persons, places, objects, and actions involved with worship are sacred.[30] They share in the extraordinary power and quality of the deity. One sanctifies oneself for worship to be able to receive even more holiness and more creative, blessing, renewing, and protecting power.

---

29. Exod 19:10–15.
30. See Fridrichsen, *Hagios-Qadoš*, 5ff.

7 | Established Orders

RITUALS AND LITURGIES

All societal action requires established rules for its development. No matter how free or charismatic or low church a religious fellowship acquires fixed forms in the space of an remarkably short time. Worship is enacted through established rites. Every religious fellowship of shared experiences, including all worship, necessarily acquires its ritual, its liturgy. In ancient times, it was considered decisively important that the rites be carried out in the "correct" manner, that "the right sacrifices be offered." The Latin term *ritus* also means that which is "right," true, legal, arranged, as it should be—that everything is done according to the most ancient law and order, the sacred institution and tradition. That the rites are correct is guaranteed by presenting them as of superhuman, divine origin.

All use of the rites—or of different ones—not based on the community's authority and fixed order is considered dangerous, harmful, evil, and a type of sorcery. It is regarded as trafficking with and use of evil, demonic, destructive forces and powers.[1]

SACRED PERSONS

To this fixed order belongs the notion that the rites should be carried out by the correct persons,[2] by those who know the rites

---

1. Cf. Mowinckel, *Psalmenstudien*, V:14–18 (Excursus).
2. Cf. Ankermann in Chantepie de la Saussaye, *Lehrbuch*, I:182ff; van der Leeuw, *Phänomenologie*, 196ff. [ET: *Religion in Essence and Manifestation*, 216–21].

and who can maintain them properly and who have the correct, sacred preparation so that the efficacy of the rites will not be wasted. All of these persons have something of the holiness and efficacy in themselves, either at certain times or permanently because of ordination. They can perform and they know. Their exercise of the rites, therefore, is correct and efficacious. Such proper persons are the king, the chief, the priest, the shaman, the oracle, and so forth. The boundaries between the types are fluid, both with regard to the perception of their kind, their preparation and their power, and with regard to the areas of their competence. The first European discoverers called the primitive religious personnel with one title—"medicine men"—because all kinds of healings were among their most important concerns. Perhaps most clearly defined is the priest, whose chief task is to attend to worship in general especially its sacrificial aspect. But he can also be a seer, as among the ancient Arabs and Hebrews. The same word which in Hebrew means sacrificial priest (*kohen*) means seer or oracle (*kahin*) in Arabic.

In Israel in the most ancient era, the head of the family or the chief of the clan was the leader of the cult. In the chief, in whom the soul and honor of the patriarch lived on, there was incorporated the holiness of the family or extended family as well as its blessing and its good fortune. The god of the tribe was, in the first place, "his" god: "the god of Abraham," "the god of Isaac," or "the god of Jacob." In addition to him there was in the most ancient era, as mentioned, the seer who besides being the mediator of oracles and prophet was also the guardian of the holy place and its "law," i.e., its proper cultic and sacral traditions and, therefore, frequently the leader and adviser of its sacrificial practices. Among the ancient Arabs and Hebrews, the roles of chief and seer could be united in one person. Moses, for example, was both leader and priest.

At the holy place of Kadesh and Sinai which gained significance when Israel's league of tribes came into existence, the seer-priests were called "Levites." After the settlement, the Levites became increasingly sacrificial priests but kept the tradition of justice, "Yahweh's justice," and mediated the technical giving of oracles with the assistance of the sacred lots, the "Urim and Thummin." Such administration of justice was called "Yahweh's conduct of justice" (*torah*). Since it was often of a sacral character, the word took on increasingly the meaning "the laws of Yahweh." In Canaan, there arose a new class of oracles or seers, the ecstatic *nabi'im* or "prophets." They had been associated with holy places and were considered to be "possessed of" or inspired by the deity. They mingled together with the old seers to form a new type. The forms were those of the old ecstatic *nabi'im*. but they took on the spirit and tradition of the seers and became. In the course of time, bearers of a genuine Yahwistic sort, bearers of religious and historical tradition which enabled them to be the foremost champions of the Yahwistic religion against the Canaanite element in the religion. The prophets could also lead (acts of) worship. During the Israelite and Judahite monarchies, the king became, as in Egypt and Babylon, the supreme person in worship and officiated at the great festivals. In daily practice the Levites, the priestly class at the temple, were his representatives. They gradually gained the exclusive right to lead worship. In Judaism, the high priest completely took over the cultic functions of the king.

SACRED SPACE

Equally important as the proper rites and persons is the proper place.[3] The holy place is such whether it permanently contains holiness or is blessed, consecrated, and dedicated for a specific occasion. Perhaps the thought was once that the place had a quality of holiness in itself and that its power emanated from it. One place can have more power than another. Examples would be a holy rock, a spring, a tree, or a mountain. The Babylonians called the temple *E-sharra*, that is to say, "the house which is full of pow-

---

3. Cf. van der Leeuw, *Phänomenologie*, 369ff. [ET: *Religion in Essence and Manifestation*, 393–402].

er." Zion is the place where there is blessing; in other words, the power of life and good fortune abide there. There "all my springs are in you" says the psalmist.[4] But it seems that the thought that dominated the religion of Israel seems equally ancient: the place is holy because the deity has "sanctified it," "dwells there," "chosen it," has permitted his name to "dwell there," "reveals himself" there, hears prayers and "blesses" there.[5] All of the traditions about holy places in the patriarchal narratives express this view. It is in such places that fellowship unfolds and is strengthened and renewed. The "covenant" is associated with the holy place, whether Kadesh, Sinai, Shechem, or Jerusalem.[6]

SACRED TIMES: THE FESTIVAL

There must be included here the proper times,[7] the "sacred times" or "time of gathering," *mo'ed* as the Israelites called it.

Time was not for the Israelites, as for us, an empty concept or a line. It consists of what happens in it.[8] But there are special turning points in time which are especially rich in content, when important things are to happen, and when it is therefore important to do that which will ensure the outcome. Such high points in time are, for example, birth, death, the beginning of a new year, of season, and so forth.[9] But that which makes these times more important or more fateful and holy than other times are, according to Israelite belief, that the deity has chosen them, sanctified them, and designated them in the very order of creation.[10]

---

4. Pss 87:7; 133:3.

5. Exod 20:24; Pss 24:5; 84.

6. Exodus 19–32; Joshua 24; Judg 9:4, 6; 2 Kings 23.

7. Van der Leeuw, *Phänomenologie*, 360ff. [ET: *Religion in Essence and Manifestation*, 388–92].

8. Cf. Pedersen, *Israel*, I–II:487–91.

9. Ibid., I–II; III–IV:281–82.

10. Gen 1:14ff.; 2:1ff.; Ps 104:19.

A holy time is a festival time. The same word that means a gathering (*mo'ed*) also means a cultic festival, synonymous with *hag*, or festival, which can also mean a place of worship.[11]

The holy time is the time where Yahweh "allows himself to be found," "makes himself known," "comes to view," and in powerful actions shows himself as he is. Then it is important to seize the opportunity on his day when the time of benevolence or grace is at hand. With the New Year Festival, there begins a new "year of benevolence." Then it is important to seek him.[12]

Which times are cultic times depends on certain conditions of life and nature and whether they make worship necessary. As a rule, these times flow with the process of the year of nature. That was the case in Israel. The chief feast of the year, called simply the "Feast of Yahweh," was an autumn or New Year's Festival, the Festival of the In-Gathering, or the Feast of Tabernacles at the full moon after the autumnal equinox when the rainy season was approaching. Another important festival was the barley harvest festival at the spring equinox and the wheat festival seven weeks later. All of these agricultural festivals were taken over from the Canaanites. The barley harvest festival occurred at approximately the same time as the ancient chief festival from the semi-nomadic times, the paschal festival. This was a feast for the slaughtering of the new lambs and a renewal of the life-force of the flock. From nomadic times also probably came the new moon festivals. The Sabbath was originally a festival of the full moon; later it meant all four "critical" days of the phases of the moon. Certain tabus, especially the forbidding of certain kinds of important work, were generally associated with those days. This distinctive Sabbath day was finally separated from its association with the phases of the moon and became an independently occurring seventh-day feast. In the course of time, it became "the

---

11. Ps 74:8.
12. Isa 49:8; 58:5; 61:2; Ps 69:13[14]; cf. Ps 65:12; Isa 55:6.

Established Orders

Lord's day," an institution of far-reaching religious and cultural blessing.[13]

DAILY SERVICE

Worship was originally something that was not part of everyday life. The sacred times are festival times at high points of life when it is necessary for life that a form of re-creation should happen. Cult originally *was* the feast. But in the course of time, the gods received their houses at the holy places. In the ancient Near Eastern states, the god became the great "king," and his temple was his "palace"—even if he also reigned on the "mountain of the god" in "the farthest north" where "heaven and earth touched" or if he dwelled in the very clouds of heaven. There he ruled as a king surrounded by his "council" and his "host." From there he sent out his servants as emissaries to carry out his work. And, like an earthly king, he was acclaimed and waited on daily by his servants. In the temple, the priests are servants of the god. Gradually, as the importance of temple worship increased in the city kingdom or capital city, daily worship developed in the temples. The priests stood day and night before his countenance and served him by clothing and anointing him, offering him food, drink, incense and music, and reciting psalms of praise and litanies. This was especially well developed in the Egyptian temples.

So was it in Jerusalem, apparently from a very early time. Even before the time of David, the "bread of the presence" was placed on a table before Yahweh and changed at certain intervals. In Jerusalem, there was the daily "morning offering," which was burned as a complete offering or holocaust in honor of Yahweh "as a pleasing odor" in his nostrils.[14] And later there was also a daily evening offering. Daily worship became a detailed ceremony that took up a great deal of the priests' time and eventually involved a large staff of subordinated temple personnel: doorkeepers, lyre

---

13. Cf. Mowinckel, *Le Decalogue*, 75ff.
14. See, for example, Gen 8:20–21; Exod 29:18; Lev 1:9.

players, singers, etc. This led to the organization of the temple personnel in an hierarchical order with the chief priest at the top. The same was done in all of the great temples of the ancient Near East.

8 | The Goals of Worship

ECSTASY

What is supposed to be gained through the cult's worshipful relationship with the deity? For us Christians, a likely answer is association with God. This is correct, but it is too broad and perhaps too specifically Christian. We must ask again, therefore, to see if it contains something concrete that can apply to all worship, even that of the Old Testament.

People in antiquity had a concrete conviction that a meeting with the deity effectively took place in worship. Their proof was being filled with an elevating and dominating feeling of power. It expressed itself in the ecstatic seizure that fellowship among the brethren brought about. They could then feel power growing in themselves. Cult and ecstasy for the ancients belonged together.[1] One sees among other proofs that the leaders of worship—the sacred persons, shamans, prophets, priests, and so forth—are often entrusted with ecstasy and must work themselves up to ecstasy in order to conduct the ritual actions. Ecstasy is for them the proof that the holy, divine power has filled them. This connection between worship and ecstatic experience was also fully clear in the gatherings of apostolic Christianity with their speaking in tongues and similar phenomena. We see this also even today in the Laestadian movement or in the Pentecostal assemblies. There the spirit has filled them. When the most ancient prophets in Israel spoke about the spirit of God and how it had come upon

---

1. Cf. van der Leeuw, *Phänomenologie*, 196ff. and s.v. "Ekstase." [ET: *Religion in Essence and Manifestation*, 217–21 and s.v. "Ecstasy"].

them, they were thinking, first of all, of its ecstatic effects. The cries and words that they uttered were considered the ecstatic word of God that disclosed the future and indeed affected what was to happen.[2]

The ecstatic feeling of jubilation about having experienced something great and important and holy was not reserved for the leaders of the cult. It was, after a fashion, the experience of the assembly. "Singing and dancing" they came from having drunk from the waters of life there where they flowed. "The joy [ecstatic feeling of jubilation] of Yahweh is your strength," the festive community was told, even in later Judean times.[3] And, on the basis of the "primitive" perception of the relationship between cause and effect, it is completely natural to bring about the meeting (with the deity) by ecstatic means: music, dancing, asceticism, and the like.[4] On a higher level of religion, all of them are regarded as divinely arranged "sacramental" means through which the deity gives his power and abilities to others.

In the meaning of the word 'ecstasy' there lies no perception of anything abnormal or psychologically unhealthy or inferior. The word denotes the open-to-all gathering around a single experience and a dominating perception and an intensity of feelings and abilities that follow with it when all other inhibiting feelings are shut off for a while, and only this one feeling fills the soul.

---

2. See Lindblom, *Profetismen i Israel*, 121ff.; and s.v. "Ekstase" [See ET: *Prophecy in Ancient Israel*, 4–6, 122–37]); Mowinckel "Ekstatiske Innslag i Profetenes Opplavelser." 135ff. [ET: "Ecstatic Experience and Rational Elaboration in Old Testament Prophecy"]. That ecstasy should itself be contained in the cultic encounter with the holy, as is the opinion of Raknes, *Mnt-Pt med det heilage*, rests on a total misunderstanding of the difference between content and form.

3. Neh 8:10.

4. Clear examples among the Israelite prophets are 1 Sam 10:5–6 and 2 Kgs 3:15. Cf. Mowinckel "Ekstatiske Innslag i Profetenes Opplavelser." 143 [ET: "Ecstatic Experience and Rational Elaboration in Old Testament Prophecy"].

The Goals of Worship

LIFE

But ecstasy is not the heart of the matter. It is a symptom, the evidence that the deity is present and at work. What happens then? What is one seeking from this?

If we look in the Bible for a single word which can express what worship seeks, then we meet both in the Old and the New Testaments the word "life." It is life that humans seek through worship, prayer, and the cultic place.[5] In the deity's holy place there is the "source of life" from which flows "the stream of life."[6] "Life" is the all-embracing expression for that which a person seeks and finds through cultic association with the holy. Life is created and given by God.[7] In order to live, humanity looks for God,[8] and God meets the humans in order to give them life.[9] This word expresses a person's highest goal, his deepest striving, and greatest value.[10] "To find life,"[11] to attain "the tree of life,"[12] "to eat the bread of life,"[13] "to drink living and life-giving water,"[14] "to travel in the land of the living,"[15] to be written in "the book of life,"[16] to be allowed to wander in "the land of the living"[17]—all of these usages try to express in one word the goal of religion and worship.

---

5. See Pedersen, *Israel*, III–IV:440–50; cf. 322–23. See also von Rad et al., ζαω; and van der Leeuw. *Phänomenologie*, 173ff. [ET: *Religion in Essence and Manifestation*, 191–205]; Heiler, *Das Gebet*, 489.

6. Pss 36:9[10]; 133:3; Ezek 47:9; cf. Prov 13:14; 14:27.

7. Genesis 1–2.

8. Amos 5:4, 6, 14.

9. Ezek 18:23; Gen 2:9; Pss 42:8[9]; 91:11, 16; Prov 3:2.

10. Ps 21:4[5].

11. Prov 8:35–36.

12. Gen 3:22; Prov 3:18, 11:30; 13:12; 15:4.

13. John 6:33, 38, 45.

14. Jer 2:13; Zech 14:8; John 4:10; 7:38.

15. Ps 16:11; Jer 21:8; Prov 5:6; 6:23; 10:17; 15:24, Acts 2:28.

16. Exod 32:32; Pss 56:8[9]; 69:28[29].

17. Isa 38:11; 53:8; Jer 11:19; Pss 27:13; 52:5[7]; 116:9; Ezek 26:20.

As a matter of fact, this applies to all other religions as well. Many of the expressions cited above also occur in them. To win and maintain life and to create life are mankind's most elementary needs. This is true even in the simplest meaning of the word. This has to do with the obtaining of food and progeny,[18] and this goal has always been part of religion's perception of life. In order to attain this goal, humanity has from the very beginning made use of both what we would call natural or rational means, and those means which are included in the expression magic. For primitive peoples, there is no boundary between the natural and the supernatural.[19] For them, magic is also something rational, as we have seen. Moreover, what we call "natural" is for the primitive filled with supernatural mysteries. But it goes without saying that at the very moment when religion becomes present and humans think of the deity, with holy powers and seeks contact with them, the first thing they seek is life. The means and actions that cause life to prosper are drawn into the religious sphere and become religious actions and means. They become cult, even if the magical concepts continue and become part of religious ones. But from this viewpoint, the religious is still not derived from magic but has rather absorbed much of it. Admittedly this involves the risk that under certain circumstances religion can become permeated by magic and drawn down into it.

To create, win, and maintain life is, then, the actual goal of worship or rituals. The psalmist also gives witness that life and the sources of life flow through the cultic place:

> How precious is your steadfast love, O God!
>   All people may take refuge in the shadow of your wings.
> They feast on the abundance of your house,
>   and you give them drink from the river of your delights.
> For with you is the fountain of life;
>   in your light we see light. (Ps 36:7–9[8–10])

---

18. Cf. Frazer, *Golden Bough*, 5.

19. Cf. van der Leeuw, *Phänomenologie*, 517 [ET: *Religion in Essence and Manifestation*, 544–45].

The Goals of Worship

But life can be perceived in many ways—more or less material or spiritual, and more 'this worldly' or more 'other worldly.' The various religions differ on this, and even in the religion of the Bible, we see a development in the perception of what 'life' is and embraces. The word and with it the cult has had a history even in the revealed religion of the Bible. Revelation in the Bible has, by and large, become a *history* of revelation. The religion of the Bible is to a marked degree an historical religion, both in the sense that it builds on historical facts as God's revealing acts and in the sense that in coming to development it has opened up its entire essence and its content in the course of a nation's history.[20]

BLESSING

In the Old Testament there is also another word that expresses what is sought through relationship to God, especially in worship: "blessing" (*berakah*).[21] In the cultic place, Yahweh promises to "come to you and bless you."[22] Jacob used the opportunity of seizing a blessing from the deity when he struggled the whole night to grasp the deity at the Jabbok Brook.[23] The Levites, i.e., the priests, had as their task "to stand before Yahweh, to minister to him, and to bless in his name."[24] The last clause expresses the intention of the whole service—to bring blessing from Yahweh to the community. The worship service climaxes in the priestly words of blessing.[25] In order to win and strengthen blessing in all its forms,[26] Israel—both as a community and as individual persons—sought out the holy place and worshipped there.

---

20. Cf. Mowinckel, *Det Gamle Testament soms Guds ord*, 23–37. [ET: *The Old Testament as Word of God*].

21. Gen 14:19–20; Exod 20:24; Num 6:23; Deut 10:8; 21:5; Pss 24:5; 118:26; 129:8. Cf. Mowinckel, *Psalmenstudien* V; Pedersen, *Israel*, III–IV, s.v. "blessing."

22. Exod 20:24.

23. Gen 32:23–32.

24. Deut 10:8.

25. Num 6:22–27.

26. Cf. Pedersen, *Israel*, I–II:182–212; and III–IV, s.v. "blessing."

Blessing embraces both what we would call the material and the spiritual, but first of all and at bottom, blessing is life, health, and fertility for people, livestock, fields, and all those things on which life literally is built. It is through worship and its rites that blessing is created, maintained, and increased, both for the community and the individual.

Blessing was the foundation of life itself. In the Old Testament we find traces of an older perception that in the mutual fellowship of God and the community in worship increased blessing is created, not only for the community but also for the deity itself. Worship increases the power of the divine to bless. The congregation not only obtains a blessing from Yahweh, but it "blesses Yahweh himself." In the Psalms, we constantly find the command "to bless Yahweh," and in and through the cultic offering of praise, the community "gives" Yahweh "honor and power" (Ps 29:1). At one time, this was literally meant.[27] Similarly, it was the priestly blessing that turned the sacrificial meat into something that was efficacious and creative of blessing—a sacramental sacrificial meal.[28] But in later Israel, these expressions took on a new meaning. To "bless Yahweh" meant to thank and praise him, and to "give him honor and power" meant to further his renown in the world and thereby extend his sphere of power. Israel's God is not dependent on the blessing of humans; rather, he is himself the source of all blessing.

Blessing is a power in the soul, a force which dwells in the family and its individual members. The ordinary just man ("justified") is at the same time the man who is blessed, and from his blessing there flows blessing to all to whom he belongs. The clan lives in the blessing of its chief and the nation in that of its king. But they have this power only because they have fellowship with Yahweh and continually maintain and renew it in the cult. The blessed one for Israel is no longer the person with much

---

27. See Mowinckel, *Psalmenstudien*, V:27–30.
28. Ibid., 24ff.; 2 Sam 9:13.

The Goals of Worship

mana in himself. He is the one "blessed by Yahweh." "The name of Yahweh" is the power that creates blessing.

The high esteem expressed in the word "holy" becomes a power of blessing and shares the power of life. This is seen also in Israel, among other ways in the old custom of swearing an oath by laying one's hand on the genitals of the partner in the contract.[29] The oath is sworn always by something holy with whose power the maker of the oath is filled. But also here we see how Yahweh steps to the fore and replaces the impersonal force of life. Even in this instance, the oath is offered in "the name of Yahweh."

It is conceivable that there was once a time—somewhere, sometime—when people undertook the activities of increasing and renewing life as things that were purely "rational." Naturally, we mean "rational" as seen from the magical view of the primitive mentality. They were seen as rational ways of producing life, fertility, growth, and prosperity. But precisely because life and the forces of life have everywhere been regarded as the most mysterious, awe-inspiring and important aspects of all reality, so have they been drawn into the sphere of the holy, the sphere of religion. Life, life-force, and blessing have become something holy. They have their source in the Holy One, in the deity. He is the creator and the sustainer of life. This thought is spread out over the whole world, even in the most primitive religions. The Canaanites knew that the deity created and renewed the world—and even that he himself was renewed in worship.[30] And Israel at a very early point took over the thought of the deity who creates and transferred it to Yahweh. Yahweh, "the living God" "who never dies" (Jer 10:10; 1 Tim 1:17), creates life and creates ever again the world he has once created. In worship, the Israelites met Yahweh who creates and gives life and blessing and thereby maintains the world.

---

29. Gen 24:2; Cf. Pedersen, *Der Eid bei den Semiten*, 150ff. For the oath as an action by which one fills himself with holy power, see Pedersen, *Israel*, III–IV:450.

30. See Hvidberg, *Graad og Latter* [ET: *Weeping and Laughter*].

ETERNAL LIFE

But at this point, one more thing must be said. In the Old Testament and in the cult of Israel, the question of eternal life was not yet present. In other words, the expression is used but the word means something different than what it means in late Judaism or in Christianity. In the Old Testament, "life" does not mean eternal life for the individual. Rather, it is the life of the community, the clan, or the nation that shall be made secure for eternity, not in an absolute philosophical sense, but so far as thought or wish could extend. It shall be secured precisely through the cult by creating and gaining new life-forces through it whenever necessary. This happens at the high points of life that recur at regular intervals, as we shall see shortly. When the king is wished "eternal life" in the Psalms and in the cultic words of blessing,[31] it is not as an individual—for an individual can have only a very long and rich life[32]—but as the representative and incorporation of the royal clan and nation or community. For the individual, worship aims at gaining life-force and the enrichment of life, and at warding off all evil powers that threaten him through sickness and impurity. It is intended to snatch him away from the threatening danger of death, the jaws of death, so that he need not risk going to the kingdom of the dead before "half their days."[33]

After death, there is in Israelite and early Jewish thought only a suspended, shadowy existence in the realm of the dead—in Sheol, the home of the dead, or in "the grave." This meshes with the usual perception of most ancient religions. The dead does not cease to exist but simply changes his form of existence.[34] Most often his is seen as a more limited form of existence. The dead person has lost his life force. "A living dog is better than a

---

31. Ps 21:4[5].
32. Pss 49:7[8]; 90:3–5.
33. Ps 55:23[24].
34. Cf. van der Leeuw, *Phänomenologie*, 111ff. [ET: *Religion in Essence and Manifestation*]; Widengren, *Religionens Värld*, 283–84.

The Goals of Worship

dead lion," said the Israelites (Eccl 9:4). "Rather a hapless serf on earth than the king of Hades" said the dead shadow of Achilles (*Odyssey* 11). Whether it is the body or the soul that continues to exist is not a vital question. Even the soul's continued existence in the kingdom of the dead is bound to the body's resting in the grave. In any event, the bones seem immortal. Hence the custom of the Egyptians, the Peruvians, certain Australian Aborigines, and others of mummifying corpses so that they could last "eternally." But this existence depends on worship. The dead person must be continually "venerated," "tended," and supplied with his needs. If certain burial rituals are not carried out in the right way and the dead provided with his veneration, which is often peaked with an annual banquet with the living—as in the Greeks' All Souls Day Festival of Anthesteria—then the existence of the dead could become even more limited. The soul would then have to wander as a restless ghost and gather morsels of food in the gutter and haunt the living, as the Babylonian Gilgamesh epic says (*Gilgamesh Epic* XII:143–154). Even the life of the dead is dependent on worship.

Other religions view the life of the dead more optimistically. Among the Persians, the soul went to an other-worldly paradise to live there in majesty and happiness[35] when the rites of the dead were properly celebrated. The pharaoh of the Egyptians and the great Egyptian citizens went after death to Osiris, the god of life and death, and became one with him. In the course of time, this also became the lot of the common Egyptians. Or pharaoh ascended to the sun and was united with the sun god in his daily journey from the land of the dead to the land of the living. The dead received a share in the mysterious sources of life. In any case, individual dead persons, such as the king or the father of the clan, can be perceived as much more powerful and wise than any living persons. They become divine. They are united with the force of life which every spring rises up from the dead earth

---

35. Cf. Nyberg in *Illustreret Religlonshistorie*, 481–82. On the burial rites, see Lehman in Chantepie de la Saussaye, *Lehrbuch*, I:248–49.

and manifests itself in the renewal of the group. Through them, the descendants and the community benefit. But this also is dependent on the proper cult of the dead. It is the rites of the dead which effectively turn pharaoh into Osiris. Without the cult of the dead, even the power of the great deceased ones dwindles.[36]

Life in the Israelite perception of life and the cult is in the first instance the life of the clan, the nation, and the individual here on earth, "in the land of the living." Nevertheless, both in ancient Israel and in other religious cults gaining eternal life could be spoken of. In the cycle of life, life and death meet, and from death new life constantly arises.[37] The old Egyptian and the Semitic religions and especially the Canaanite cult were built clearly on the basic thought that life and death are only shifting aspects of one and the same thing. The god of the dead, Mot (Death), was also the god of life and fertility. He is the grain of wheat which is sown, harvested, ground, milled, baked and becomes alive and indeed creates life.[38]

The oldest semi-nomadic Israel had concepts of life arising from the land of the dead through the "living water" of the springs. They thought also of the power-creating "wisdom" which was revealed through an oracle at a holy spring, such as the "source of judgment" at Kadesh on the Sinai Peninsula.[39] They knew that the souls of the dead were "the ones who knew" (*yed'onim*) whom the living asked for efficacious advice.[40] They knew also that power and blessing were to be found at the graves of their ancestors. Even the Israelites called the dead a "divine

---

36. On the Egyptian view of Pharaoh as Osiris, and on the cult of the dead, see Frankfort, *Kingship and the Gods*, 110ff., 181ff.; Sander-Hansen in *Illustreret Religlonshistorie*, 115ff.

37. Cf. Kristensen, *Livet fra dødet*; and *Tro eller Overtro*, 16ff.

38. Cf. Hvidberg, *Graad og Latter* [ET: *Weeping and Laughter*].

39. Exod 15:25; 17:1–7; Cf. Gen 14:7. See Mowinckel. "Kadesj, Sinai og Jahve."

40. Lev 19:31; 20:6, 27; Deut 18:11; 1 Sam 28:3, 9; 2 Kgs 21:6; Isa 8:19; 19:3. Cf. 1 Samuel 21.

being" (*'elohim*).⁴¹ Therefore, "veneration" of the dead ancestors and relatives, "care" for them, and "service" to them belonged to the essence of cult, even in the ancient Semitic religions. The ancestors in the grave were to be venerated with food, drink, and equipment in order that they could maintain their extraordinary "divine" power and let it stream down to their descendants through fellowship in the graveside meal. Such was the case also in ancient Israel.⁴²

To be sure, these thoughts receded in the religion of Yahweh, since Yahweh stood in such opposition to the indigenous gods of life and death. For this reason, the world of the dead in later Israel was separated so sharply from the land of the living that everything associated with the dead was considered to be unclean. The true believers insisted that Yahweh, as "the living God," had nothing to do with the world of the dead or dead persons. "He does no wondrous thing there and the shadows do not stand up in order to praise him."⁴³ In the religion of Yahweh, it is the eternal life of the clan and the nation, its constantly experienced deliverance from death, and its renewal to new power by Yahweh's epiphany in the land of the living are also so renewed.

---

41. 1 Sam 28:13.

42. The graves of the fathers lie at sacred shrines (Gen 35:8; 50:10-11; Num 20:1, 22-29; Josh 24:30; Judg 2:9; 10:25; 12:7, 10, 12, 15; 16:1; 1 Sam 10:2; Jer 31:13). This means that they were themselves originally sacred places, as is the case to this day in the Semitic world. See Stade, *Biblische Theologie des Alten Testaments*, 1:110-11. On the connection between graves of the fathers and the basic meaning of the cult of the fathers among the Bedouins in Arabia, much information is to be had from the work of Musil, *Arabia Petraea* III. Cf. also Pedersen in *Illustreret Religlonshistorie*, 159, 160, 203ff. The cult of the fathers appears again in the cult of the saints and of the well. "No arbitrary command can prevent the people from seeking out power from the place where experience has shown then that it is to be found," i.e., at the graves of the fathers (ibid., 203). Birkeli has done important research on the ancestor cult in Scandinavia. This material has been brought together in the popular book *Fedrekult*. For the ancestor cult in Madagascar, see Ruud, *Guder og Fedre*. For a general treatment, consult Birkeli, *Religlonshistorie*, I:106ff.

43. Pss 6:5[6]; 30:9[10]; 88:10-12[11-13]; 115:17.

The idea of eternal life in the full meaning of the word for the individual arose late in Judaism and then as belief in *resurrection* from the grave with a renewal of the dead and decomposing body. In this action and with it, the soul also woke to life again. As is well known, this belief was not universally held in Judaism at the time of Jesus. The school or sect of the Sadducees, which denied the resurrection, represented here the conservative branch of theology; it can hardly be doubted that belief in the resurrection in Judaism received an impetus from Persian religion. But all the foundation was laid for this in older Judaism.

That Yahweh had the power to make a dead person come alive—and sometimes did so—this was something that ancient Israel was fully aware of. In reality, he did so every time he made a sick person healthy. For the sick person was, according to Hebraic thought, one who had "death in himself." Sheol had him in its jaws. The flood of the realm of death had "reached up to his throat." Then Yahweh came and snatched him away from the claws of death, "drew him up from the deep," "from the waters," "from the swamp." Yahweh can do anything he wishes. Therefore, belief in resurrection could easily develop in late Judaism.

That the fate of the dead was regarded as dependent on cultic measures by their survivors is seen in Maccabees where the military commander Judas had a collection taken and prayers offered for those who had fallen in battle.

From Judaism, the belief in the resurrection passed over into Christianity and Islam. In Christianity, the connection between worship and eternal life received another twist. We see it most clearly in the Gospel of John. Eternal life, or "life"—which here is also a central theme—arrives with the life and spiritual fellowship with Christ. "And this is eternal life, that they may know you, the only true God, and Jesus Christ whom you have sent" (John 17:3). This life exists already. Eternal life is a reality that has begun here. But the Gospel of John knows that the fellowship of life and death with Christ is experienced presently and really in the cultic fellowship of the community in the Lord's

The Goals of Worship

Supper. The community is the body of Christ. In it, Christians have fellowship with the Lord's death, resurrection, and life, as we hear from Paul. This is actualized in the Lord's Supper where participation in the resurrection and eternal life are anticipated. But even in Christianity, the older, more "material" and concrete thoughts about the dependency of life on worship emerge again. Among the older Greek theologians, the Eucharistic meal was considered a "medicine of immortality" (*pharmakon aphthanasias*, see Ignatius of Antioch, *To the Ephesians* 2:20). The "last anointing" of the Roman church is a cultic action with a view toward eternal life.

9 | The Cycle
The Renewal of Life

What happens in the cult, then, is that life, blessing, fertility, prosperity, "peace," and "good fortune" are created for the people, the livestock and fields, and body as well as soul. Life and its foundation are renewed.

This is a necessary occurence. There are certain high points in time when life is especially threatened, and it is important to save it, to secure it, to strengthen it, to increase it. Or there are certain high points where it is especially important to get it to flow richly and strongly, when it needs to be sanctified and hallowed. All transitions in the cycle of life are such important points: the transition from winter to spring, from dry season to rainy season, birth, initiation to the community of adults, weddings, war, the settlement of peace, and so forth. At all such points, more or less comprehensive cultic arrangements must take place for the whole community, the clan, or the household.[1]

Humans see that life and blessing are closely related to the cycle of nature, to the sun and the spring, or to the rainy season and the flood. One sees that life dies gradually as the height of the summer and the dry season progress or when the winter causes everything to freeze. In life, there are evil powers as well as good.[2] Death and the powers of death, "the curse," stand in constant opposition to blessing and life. And there are times when it seems as though the powers of death are winning. Outside of

---

1. Cf. A van Gennep, *Les Rites de passage* [ET: *Rites of Passage*]; van der Leeuw, *Phänomenologie*, 173ff. [ET: *Religion in Essence and Manifestation*, 192–204]; Birket-Smith, *Kulturens Veje*, 2:94ff. [ET: *Paths of Culture*].

2. Cf. Pedersen, *Israel*, I–II:411–52, 453–96.

The Cycle

the world of life and blessing there lies the world of death and curse, the desert, the wasteland, and sometimes it threatens to break into the land of life and lay waste to it. This thought then was as alive among the ancient Israelites[3] as among the ancient Scandinavians.[4] When the mid-summer of the Near East devastates the earth, then death has prevailed over life. Mot (Death) has prevailed over the lord of life (Ba'al), but Ba'al can rise again and crush Mot. This was the fundamental thought and the basic experience in the ancient Canaanite religion and cult.[5]

But similar thoughts have also gone over into the religion of Israel. Yahweh, to be sure, cannot really be conquered. "Are you not from of old . . . ? You shall not die."[6] But he too is constantly engaged in battle against the evil powers that will destroy the world that he has made. The curse can always threaten to prevail over the blessing. In the autumn, chaos again threatens to prevail over the cosmos. Yahweh must intrude, therefore, and he does this through the cult.

Humans know also that life and crops cannot grow of themselves. In order that the soil can produce and the human life can continue, important things must be done. If the life of nature does not prevail, life itself cannot continue. In the earliest times, it was not self-evident that a rainy season followed a dry season. It was a new insight that the narrator in the Bible had when he saw that the regular turning of the year's seasons are founded in God's own covenant promise,[7] and that the frequent droughts in Canaan were caused by God's wrath and punishment.[8] When the year is over, the world is on the point of dying. It must then be

---

3. Ibid., 354ff.
4. Cf. Grønbech, *Vaar Folkaeet i Oldtiden*, 2:2ff.
5. Cf. Hvidberg, *Graad og Latter* [ET: *Weeping and Laughter*].
6. Hab 1:12. The ordinary biblical text has been changed on doctrinal grounds by the Jewish scribes as also by our translators. But the tradition among the scribes (*massora*) shows clearly how the text was originally read.
7. Gen 8:22.
8. 1 Kgs 17:1.

provided with new force or created anew in order that life may continue. The life-forces are renewed by God: "When you [God] send forth your spirit, they are created; and you renew the face of the ground," says the psalmist.[9] It is this creation, this renewal of the world—the world of the people in question—which, according to ancient thought, occurred in worship. The Babylonian myth of the fertility goddess, Ishtar, and her descent into the underworld depicted how life ceased, grain did not grow, animals did not reproduce, and men and women were infertile.[10] The world reverted to how it was before it was created.

The cultic activities, therefore, must continually be redone at the proper times. Blessing "wears out" and the world "wears out." It is renewed when worship, so to speak, sets the sacred powers in motion again, when the deity "comes" for "new salvation." Even in rabbinic Judaism it was said in a collection of the "Sayings of the Fathers" (*Pirqe Aboth*) that worship is one of the three things that maintains the world. "Sacrifice is the navel of the world," says one of the Indian Vedas or songs of sacrifice.

Also in Israel's cult these thoughts emerge. In the feast, especially the great harvest or New Year's Festival, the Feast of Tabernacles, which was in ancient times considered to be simply "Yahweh's feast." Yahweh himself comes. He "turns destiny" and creates the world anew, just as all of the powers of death and evil were threatening to overcome his people and its world. The festival was also understood as "the enthronement of Yahweh" when he came and prevailed over his enemies. Invisible, but represented by his visible symbol, the ark—his throne or his footstool—he himself was present and entered into his palace in a great festive procession with psalms and trumpets. Then he was

---

9. Ps 104:30.

10. The text is translated by Ebeling in Gressmann, *Altorientalische Texte und Bilder zum Alten Testament*, 2nd ed., 1:206ff.; Ungnad, *Religion Babyloniens und Assyriens*, 142ff.; Briem, *Babyloniska myter och sagor*, 124ff. The poem's Sumerian (Old Babylonian) original has been rediscovered and reconstructed, so far as the fragmentary texts allow, by Kramer in his *Sumerian Mythology*, 83ff.

The Cycle

seated on his throne in the temple and grasped again the royal scepter and "judged" the world, that is to say set everything in its right order. Then he turns "the cycle of the year" back again to its starting point in the beginning and everything becomes as it was in the beginning. Then he was lauded as king by his cheering people in typical enthronement psalms that begin with the "cry of royal praise": "Yahweh has become king" (e.g., Ps 96:10; 97:1). Then he revealed himself in his powerful acts and their effects. Then the rainy season began with its new blessing and fertility for land and people and livestock. Then, he gave "strength and power to his people" and "blessed his people with peace."[11] For now he triumphed again over the conquered flood, over the dragon, over the force of chaos, above which he has built his throne.[12]

Enemies are here, according to the oldest way of thinking, the very powers of death and drought, the powers of chaos in existence. Such forces are unclean; they represent "the curse" that ever grinds away at blessing and each year is at the point of making the earth desolate once again, of snuffing out life and making the world into that chaos that it was before creation. It is that which Yahweh prevents by coming in his festival.

Worship is therefore naturally connected to the year of nature, the cycle in which the life and death of nature unfolds. In Palestine, this new life began with the rainy season in the fall. Then the old year came to an end and life began anew. New Year time is universally the most important cultic season.

But here must be mentioned an important change that took place in the religion of Israel. Israel never forgot that the relationship between Yahweh and Israel had been founded through an historical event which it perceived as Yahweh's choice of Israel and his conclusion of a covenant with them. More and more, Yahweh became the god who revealed himself not only in nature

---

11. Ps 29:11.
12. Ps 29:10. See further Mowinckel, "Tronstigningssalmerne og Jahves tronstigningsfest"; and Mowinckel, *Psalmenstudien* II; [Ed: Mowinckel, *The Psalms in Israel's Worship*, 1:106–92].

and the life of nature but above all in history, in those things that actually happened. He led the life of the nations, and the kings were instruments in his hand. Through history, he led his people to that goal that he had set. He chastised them and brought them up as his children. He was the lord of history and of time. The old Canaanite designations of a deity as "the father of years" or "the god of time" originally pertained to the life of nature; but they received a new meaning in Israel, just as the expression "the living God" had received a new meaning. The greatest content of the feast in Israel, therefore, was that history became alive again. Yahweh came again and renewed the covenant with his people and thereby created it anew. In the festival, the community experienced the old salvation history anew, the delivery from Egypt, the miracle at the Red Sea, the revelation at Sinai—as new and current reality. So the religion of Israel received a truly unique stamp that distinguished it from all of the other ancient cults in the Near East.[13]

---

13. See Mowinckel, *Psalmenstudien* II:54–56, 150–78.

10 | The Creating Drama

ACTUALIZATION THROUGH PRESENTATION

The new creation in the cult happens when what is to be created is presented in the rites that are carried out and expressed through the words that are spoken. The holy must "take place" or "be presented" in order to be real.[1] The words accompany and express what is to happen in and through the cultic actions or rites. In a sense, these presentations are in keeping with the ancient presentations of self-fulfilling, "magical," efficacious rites (sympathetic magic, a bringing into being of a reality by enacting it). And since religion and cult, as we have seen, include presentations and actions that stem from the magical view of reality, they have universally adopted and adapted imitative actions that resemble and indeed often are borrowed from sympathetic and imitative magic. But there is nonetheless an essential difference. In cult, the idea of the deity's personally involved and working power is the fundamental starting point. The deity works through these things. Hence, the rites are symbols that express and signify what is going to happen, and thus, through them, it does happen. Both the imitative dance and all kinds of festive processions that play such a great role in cult have, as a rule, this actualizing aspect.[2] They illustrate what is happening in the cult, and through them, it happens. Through the war dance, for ex-

---

1. Cf. van der Leeuw, *Phänomenologie*, 425ff. [ET: *Religion in Essence and Manifestation*, 447–53].

2. See, for example, Hooke, ed., *Myth and Ritual*, 22, 24, 27, 130–31, 188 and elsewhere.

ample, the victory over the enemy is created. Through the strong and often ecstatic feeling that the dancers experience being filled with an extraordinary, holy power, they are convinced of the deity's presence and strength.[3]

Reality is experienced by participating in that which is presented. Reality is already present as a spiritual reality, as a power in the soul that must be transformed into real action and result. The creation of the world happens when it is portrayed, for example, as a battle between life and death. In this presentation, the deity himself is present, wins, and creates. In the cult of Canaan, there was presented and experienced the victory of Ba'al over Mot, or death. Israel also had, in one or another form, taken on a more or less symbolic presentation of Yahweh's battle and victory in his cult. This is occasionally suggested in the festive psalms.[4]

The cult has, then, always a more or less clear, dramatic stamp. It is a cultic drama. This can have a more or less realistic or symbolic form. In the cult, that which happens is presented visibly through dramatic rites and symbols. Here we mean the arrival and presence of the deity and his battle and victory over the evil powers and with that his creation and foundation of the reality on which the community lives. The cult becomes action and reaction. It is an event and a libretto which interprets and reacts to the event.

The dramatic aspect appears especially in all forms of nature and fertility cults. That which should happen is presented in efficacious rites, words, and symbols and thereby becomes reality. In the ritual dances of North and Central American Indian tribes are symbolized and presented the growth and life of the nourishing plants and animals; thereby an abundance of maize or soybeans or buffalo or whatever is created.[5] In Egypt, one acted out

---

3. On the cultic dance, see Oesterley, *The Sacred Dance*.

4. Pss 46:8–9[9–10]; 48:8–9[9–10].

5. For example, the sun-dance of the Arapao Indians, see Dorsey, *The Arapao Sun Dance*; the Oraibi winter solstice festival, see Dorsey and Voth, *The Oraibi-Soval*; and for the summer snake festival, see Voth, *The Summer*

The Creating Drama

on the great day of the Festival of Osiris the journey of Osiris to the grave, his son Horus' victorious battle against the enemy Seth and Osiris' resurrection to a new life. The community itself participated in the battle and that which happened. For them, too, the outcome of the battle meant victory over the powers of death, the resurrection of vegetation, and new, rich life.[6] In vast parts of West Asia in ancient times, there was a common cultic pattern in rich detail that was especially bound to the cultic feast of the New Year. The chief features, which were repeated were more or less clearly in different places, were the presentation of the death and resurrection of the god, re-enactment of the creation myth, the ritual battle between the god and his enemies, the god's "sacred marriage" with the mother goddess or fertility goddess, the great festive procession that presents the god's triumphant march as victorious king and his entry into his castle followed by the other gods and his whole community, his people.[7] The Marduk Festival in Babylonia, presented Marduk's victory over the primeval sea and over the powers of chaos, Tiamat, the dragon of the primeval sea, and the reading was the creation epic, which described the battle and what it signified: the creation of an ordered world.[8]

In fertility cults, the basic thought appeared especially clearly in festivals of the god Tammuz, the god of vegetation. In ritual songs of lament, one wept over his death and departure and depicted the wasted and destructive condition that his departure had brought upon the land and the powers of chaos and

---

Snake Ceremony. See the comprehensive survey by Grønbech in *Illustreret Religionshistorie*, 2nd ed., 67ff.

6. See Erman, *Ägyptische Religion*, 2nd ed., 63ff. See also the very insightful, clear and lucid presentation by Henri Frankfort, *Kingship and the Gods*, especially the analysis and description of the customary feast (79ff.) and of the "installation mystery play" (123ff.).

7. See Hooke, ed., *Myth and Ritual*, 8; but notice Frankfort's caution against exaggeration, op. cit., 382 n. 5; cf. 405 n. 1.

8. See the bibliographical references in Mowinckel, *Psalmenstudien*, II:26–35; and especially Frankfort's analysis of the New Year Festival in Babylon, *Kingship and the Gods*, 313ff., and of the "sacred marriage," 295ff.

the devastation of the primeval sea or of drought. The rites and texts presented the journey of his beloved, the goddess Ishtar, to the realm of death to bring him back. His resurrection was greeted with hymns of jubilation. The wasteland was again created to a world, a cosmos, a fertile, cultivated land and home for human beings and for animals.[9]

In Ugarit, in Phoenicia, in Israel's nearest neighbor, we find the same basic thought and the same type of cultic drama. Here participants in the cult experienced the battle between Alyan-Ba'al and the god of death, Mot, Ba'al's death and Mot's victory. We encounter the battle and victory over Mot by the beloved of Ba'al, "the virgin" Anat, Ba'al's resurrection and enthronement as the king of gods and men, the rebuilding and the rededication of his temple, his sacred marriage with the virgin Anat and the reflourishing of vegetation. All of these were accompanied by songs of lament, songs of jubilation and epic texts that explained and symbolized by partly drastically realistic fertility rites.[10] Thus were fertility for life and people and flock and earth secured.

The basic object that was actualized in this cultic drama is, in a word, "salvation" or "width" or "roominess"—which the Hebrew word for salvation (*yesha'*) actually means. Salvation means that land and people are torn from the power of death and chaos and that life and the world are created anew. The thought and myth of creation play a chief role in many of these cultic dramas. They deal with the entire world of the people to whom they are relevant. Their "land" represented the world for them. In Hebrew, the word *'erets* means both world and land. It is the creation of the world that happens once again. Both drama and salvation are on a cosmic scale. The world is saved from chaos and becomes cosmos once again. The cultic drama is a dramatic presentation and experiencing of "salvation history," a new realization of it.

9. Cf. in Witzel, *Tammuz Liturgien und Verwandtes*.

10. Cf. Hvidberg, *Graad og Latter* [ET: *Weeping and Laughter*]; Pedersen in *Illustreret Religionshistorie*, 198ff.

The Creating Drama

THE FESTIVE DRAMA IN ISRAEL

The cult of ancient Israel and certainly the chief festival of the year, the autumn or New Year Festival, also had much of the same stamp and in reality was built on the same cultic drama, although with essential changes. It was built on the same influence from the same cultic drama. We have many indications for this both in occasional hints of individual influences and in the idea that even in late Jewish times were associated with the New Year Festival. One important piece of evidence is a group of psalms, the so-called "enthronement psalms," which depict the battle and victory of Yahweh over the primeval sea, the dragon and his other enemies; his coming and his epiphany at his enthronement as king; his creation of the world; the kingship that he has just entered; and his triumphal procession at the head of his people into the newly dedicated temple.[11] These psalms must, without doubt, be interpreted as a witness to a corresponding feast. The feast is that of Yahweh's enthronement, where all these events were presented through dramatic symbols in the rituals of cult. The festival is nothing other than the well-known autumn, New Year, and Tabernacle Festival. It is Yahweh's day above all others, the day of his epiphany and the day of his enthronement. It is a new phase of the festival and especially of its climax on the last day, "the final, great day of the festival time." These psalms give us awareness that the festival celebrates Yahweh as victorious lord over the dragon, the primeval sea, and over all his enemies, as creator of the world, as king and ruler of the world, and as his people's just and saving guide. The festival hymns praise him for all these actions of salvation but especially as the lord who has now become king. The cry of royal praise "Yahweh has become king!" is their characteristic phrase. The high point of the festival was the great and dramatically arranged festival procession, in which Yahweh's personal presence at the head of his people was symbolized by his sacred box, the ark, which again was borne

---

11. See Mowinckel, *Psalmenstudien*, II:89–94.

into his palace where he was thought to reign invisibly on the throne of the cherubim inside in the holy of holies. There the eye of faith could be opened and see him, as the prophet Isaiah on such a feast day was permitted to see him "sitting on a lofty and elevated throne and the skirt of his robe filled the entirety of the holy place." The psalms point to symbolic rites that have presented his victorious battle.

> Come, behold the works of Yahweh;
> > see what desolations he has brought on the earth.
> He makes wars cease to the end of the earth;
> > he breaks the bow and shatters the spear;
> > he burns the shields with fire. (Ps 46:8–9[9–10])

> As we have heard, so have we seen
> > in the city of Yahweh of hosts,
> in the city of our God,
> > which God establishes forever. (Ps 48:8[9])

All cult has in fact, more or less clearly, this dramatic aspect. It presents something important and fundamental to life that "happens." What happens in the cult thereby happens also in reality. It is not by accident that both the Greek drama and the Christian mystery plays of the Middle Ages grew directly out of worship. Even in the festive worship of the church, this drama is valid: the reenactment, re-experiencing, and new realization of the basic facts of salvation. Especially in many of the Christmas and Easter hymns, the eternal "today" stands out clearly. "Today a savior is born to us," or "three women went out this morning, they came back with gladsome tide."[12]

But we see an essential difference between the cultic drama of Israel and that of the other ancient Near Eastern religions. In the other Near Eastern religions, and not least of all in that of Canaan, the god was to a great degree regarded as being one with nature. The death and reawakening of nature to life was thought

---

12. The *Landstad Revised Hymnal*, #114; originally #349 (which surprisingly enough is discontinued in *The Landstad Revised Hymnal*). Cf. also Brorson's Magnificent Psalm of the Ascension *Landstad Revised Hymnal*, #405.

of and presented as the god's death and resurrection. This idea was totally foreign to the religion of Israel. Israel can, to be sure, have taken over much of the general Near Eastern cultic pattern and the concepts and rites that went along with it. But Yahweh is "the God that lives," "the holy God that does not die."[13] That which is essential in the cultic festival is that "he *comes*" and makes himself visible.[14] He shows in recreating and conquering action who he is.[15] Israel's cult was a confrontation with the almighty, the god already well-known from the experience of history who comes to his own and creates blessing, wellbeing and "peace," victory, and good fortune. He gives to his people that which is required in the struggle of life.

And while in the other Near Eastern religions the elementary demands of life—the fertility and strength of nature and of the people—were made secure, created anew, and experienced in worship—in part with literal sexual abandon—in the religion of Israel an historical element came to the fore. The foundation of life was, for Israel, God's choice of this people and his covenant with them, his people's "creation" through the marvelous experiences of the exodus from Egypt and conquest of Canaan and victories over the indigenous kings and people. This also, then, was experienced, confirmed, and actualized anew by Yahweh's coming in the cultic festival. The future existence of the people was assumed through Yahweh's creative coming, by which victory over all historical, hostile powers was confirmed and made certain. Yahweh's coming was itself the victory; it was salvation, and in the symbolism of the cultic drama, this battle and victory were also expressed. Therefore, we see that the New Year or Enthronement Festival psalms also present the fundamental historical facts of salvation: Israel's creation by election and liberation from Egypt, and the foundation of the Yahweh cult in Zion and the building of the temple as something that "occurs"

---

13. Hab. 1:12 (see above p. 73 n. 6).
14. Pss 96:13; 98:9.
15. Ps 76:2.

again in the festival. One of the psalms (Psalm 132) is the text for a dramatic performance in festal procession where David and his men again appear and search for the ark of the covenant, which had been lost in battle with the Philistines. In the festal procession they bring it to Jerusalem, "the place where Yahweh will dwell," and where he now blesses his people and its king "for the sake of David his servant."

RE-ENACTMENT OF THE FACTS AND HISTORY OF SALVATION

The experience of the cult, then, becomes a re-enactment and re-experiencing of the fundamental act that happened at the very beginning. That "salvation"—that is creation, the new life of nature, emergence as a people, and so forth—was ever repeated in the cult. This is what is involved in the idea that the festival is celebrated "to bring to mind" the exodus from Egypt and so forth.

The essential thing about the cultic drama is that it does not merely portray for consideration or memory, but rather that it is a *creative* drama. It is not a play for the education of the people, but something really happens in it. The drama that takes place is that God comes and meets humanity in its situation and with the display of his wondrous power in battle and victory creates a new situation for them. That which is created through this meeting is nothing less than all of the reality that the community or assembly needs in order to live. This includes the natural, historical and the spiritual realities among which, of course, the ancients did not distinguish. It is "life" in its fullest. Moreover, the spiritual "benefits of salvation," which more and more in the higher religions become the focal point, are present in it. It is all of existence in its fluctuating rhythms that is newly created in the cultic drama; it is the world. It is, therefore, the cultic drama that is an actual reliving and re-experiencing of whatever happened in the beginning. The re-experiencing in Israel included the cosmic reality and the historical, Yahweh's victory over the forces of chaos and his basic victory over all of Israel's enemies in the exodus and in their taking of the land.

CREATION OF THE FUTURE

In the cultic festival, it is the past that is reenacted and the future that is created. Peace and salvation, victory, well-being, good fortune, and security in the new "year of benevolence" that lies at hand are founded and guaranteed in worship of the New Year Festival. Faith anticipates the future. The past, present, and future blend together in the "today" of the festal experience. That which is being created is not already visible; the festival is to secure the time that is to come. This is valid both for the Australian Aborigines' ceremonies and the nature and fertility cult feasts. The coming of the deity, his "advent," in the festival also includes expectation. The time of advent is the time of expectation. Israel's New Year Festival was held before the rainy season began and created the world anew. It was intended to make certain that the rainy season came. The festival was a thanksgiving for the year that had been and a festival to initiate the year that was to be. That which was to come was seen in pictures and colors of the festive myth. Just as Yahweh had won the victory over chaos, so should he now in the contemporary situation win a victory over all evil powers and all of Israel's enemies and make his kingdom secure.

And therefore we see that even after Israel had collapsed as a kingdom, the hope of a new "day of Yahweh" lived on. Yahweh had not been overcome by the gods of the gentiles. The proclamation of the prophets had made Yahweh too large in the eyes of the people that he could be so seen. He had not forgotten his covenant. When the time of punishment was over, he would again have his day. Judaism lived for centuries on this hope of restoration. And so we see that the hope took content and coloration directly from the experience in worship on the royal day of Yahweh. The restoration was to be a new enthronement day for Yahweh when he would again establish his kingdom. The power of the world was likened to the power of chaos. Salvation was depicted in pictures and colors from the battle of enthronement and the consequent victory, deliverance, and the new creation. From the experiences of the Enthronement Festival and its ideas, Judaism's eschatology received its concrete notions.[16]

---

16. See Mowinckel, *Psalmenstudien*, II:211, 324 [Ed.: Mowinckel, *The Psalms in Israel's Worship*, 1:189–92].

11 | Prophecy and Mysticism

CULTIC ECSTASY AND CULT PROPHETS

In the cult, there is experienced the most intimate connection with the deity. The participants are filled with "holy power," with "blessing." They experience the personal coming and presence of the deity. They experience the battle and victory of life and the deity and the deity's triumph. With all their soul, they take part in what "happens." All of their feelings are subjected to the most forceful fluctuations and are raised to the greatest heights. They are lifted out of everyday concerns and the everyday world of weakness and death. They weep over the death of the god; they rejoice in ecstatic happiness over his resurrection or, as in Israel, over his triumph. The Australian Aborigines weep from divine seizure when they experience what happens in their religious ceremonies. "Tears and laughter" was for the Canaanites as well as the Israelites a comprehensive expression that embraced the festive experiences.[1] They sow with weeping so they reap with laughter, says the psalmist (Ps 126:5). The reading of the demands of the law in the New Year Festival released the congregation's deep feeling of sinfulness and caused loud crying, but this could not remain. The leaders of the cult consoled them by saying that the festive "joy of Yahweh is your strength."[2]

This last should be taken absolutely literally. Precisely the strong emotional experience, the powerful rush of feeling to the heights of ecstasy, was exactly proof that the worshippers had

1. Cf. Hvidberg, *Graad og Latter* [ET: *Weeping and Laughter*].
2. Neh 8:10.

shared in the power of the deity.³ This is the thing that causes the Australian Aborigines to weep out of "fear and trembling" in the presence of the deity. It is in the Sioux Indians' feeling that Wakanda or Manitu is present and has filled them with power for all of life's activities. It is the experience of Yahweh's personal nearness that filled the Israelites with strength, and this ecstasy is also proof both that the deity is present with his blessings and that he has strengthened his worshippers.

Both in Canaanite and Israelite worship, this led to especially seized (both in the word's subjective and objective meanings) individuals who felt themselves to be full of the deity. In Israel, one did not say that he was filled with or possessed by Yahweh, but by Yahweh's spirit, so that whatever he said or did in ecstasy was received as the deity's own speech or as his symbolic but efficacious act. Ecstatic cries could be translated as God's own speech. Whatever the ecstatics said were efficacious words that foretold and determined the future.⁴ That such foretellers (Hebrew, *nabi'*) or prophets from the very beginning were united with worship is a universal element in the world of religion. In Israel, this union presumably continued as long as temple worship continued. Both in ancient times and even so late as the time of the book of Chronicles, we hear about an organized fraternity of temple prophets who, among other things, had their word to say in the rituals of festival worship.⁵ Their task was to proclaim "the good news" at the cultic festival about Yahweh's coming and his fidelity and the blessing that he would create for his people.

The religious life and theological reflection and tradition that lived in these circles of temple prophets is the background of the "prophetic reform movement," which is one of the character-

---

3. See above, pp. 40–41.

4. Cf. Holscher, *Die Propheten*, 129ff.; above, 40.

5. See Mowinckel, *Psalmenstudien* III. [Ed. Mowinckel, *The Psalms in Israel's Worship*, 2:65–67].

istic elements that separates the religion of Israel from the other Near Eastern religions.[6]

In the religion of Israel, however, something noteworthy happened. What the cultic prophets had to say during worship was originally that which according to the prevailing belief should be said. The oldest cultic prophets in Israel spoke out according to the prevailing perception about Yahweh's covenant with Israel that bound him, so to speak, to create good fortune and victory for his people. Truly, for them, "the voice of the people was the voice of God." They proclaimed that which everyone wished, believed and expected. But both because the prophetic movement had become the bearer of the genuine Yahwistic desert traditions in opposition to the Caananized official worship, and because on the basis of these ideas they experienced Yahweh as a compelling power that they had to obey, there arose within this prophetic class men who felt obliged to proclaim messages from Yahweh that were diametrically opposed to the official and popular religion. They became bearers of the progressive line in the religion of revelation. This could lead, among other things, to the cultic prophets becoming critics and judges of worship. They appeared at the cultic festivals, but they came to proclaim what people had not expected of them and did not wish to hear—judgment and defeat instead of good fortune and victory. They became proclaimers of belief and obedience and morality instead of heralds of the good fortune attendant on worship and daily life.

CULTIC MYSTICISM AND THE SPECULATIVE MYSTICISM

There is also another essential element in the world of religion that goes together with the ecstatic experience in the cult, namely

---

6. Cf. Mowinckel, "Ekstatiske Innslag i Profetenes Opplavelser" [ET: "Ecstatic Experience and Rational Elaboration in Old Testament Prophecy"]. For the spiritual life in prophetic circles, see "Oppkomsten av Profetlitteraturen," 81ff.

mysticism.[7] In the great tension of feelings, there is experienced a unity with the deity as something that lifts people out of themselves. When ecstasy, whether in its exalted form or its subdued form, attains its highest degree, there is the experience that the consciousness of the ego is, as it were, shut off, and the boundary between the "I" and the deity, "the one," "the totality," is removed. The one seized by the deity or submerged into him is out of himself. He goes into the one, into the totality, into God. Thus, the mystic can say, "I am he" or "he is I" or "I am God." The oldest "primitive" mysticism was always associated with the cultic and ritual action's experience of unity with the divine, with the deity. In the background of this experience, there stands the psychological insight into the essence of experience and with it an awareness of how one can cause this situation, a psychology and even a technique of mysticism. The ancient mystics were the first to have speculated over the essence of the soul and its abilities. They were the first psychologists.

In this process of being lifted out of one's self, this unity with the divinity, this merging with the one, with totality, the mystic finds the meaning of life, its highest joy. In many religions, therefore, this process is separated from worship. It becomes a life that is sought and cultivated for its own sake. In its essence, mysticism is the same we encounter in India, in Christianity, or in Islam.[8] But it receives, understandably, its more or less special individual stamp from the various religions in which it occurs.

The primitive cultic mysticism of unity we meet, as we have said, in the ancient religions of the Near East and in their prophetic essence. We also see that certain forms and expressions from this concept have gone over into Israel's most ancient forms of prophecy. But against the thought that Yahweh had "gone into" the prophet or that a person could be "one with" Yahweh, genuine Yahwism reacted very early and perhaps even from the very first. The distance between Yahweh and humans is too great.

7. Cf. Andræ, *Mystikens Psykologi*, 11ff.
8. Cf. Otto, *West-östliche Mystik* [ET: *Mysticism East and West*].

Prophecy and Mysticism

Even if Yahweh has created man "in his image and likeness" and made him only "a little lower than the angels" as the poet says in Psalm 8, still there is a decisive distance between a "divine being" or "angel" and the like and Yahweh himself. Therefore, very early the thought prevailed that when the prophet in ecstasy shared in the divinity so it was not Yahweh himself who "filled" him, but it was "Yahweh's spirit" and his wonder-working power that performed the action. "The spirit" was regarded in part as a wonder working power and in part as a personified essence that "entered into" and spoke through the prophet. But even this perception was gradually "rationalized." The prophet felt himself to be, first of all, Yahweh's ambassador, his messenger, who brought Yahweh's messages. The messenger formula—"thus says Yahweh: speak to so and so"—became the routine introduction to the prophetic word. "The word" was the gift with which the prophet was sent.[9] Israel's prophets were not mystics, and mysticism in the truest meaning of the word really has no place in the religion of the Old Testament.

---

9. Cf. Mowinckel, "'Anden' og 'Ordet' hos de Foreksilske Profeter" [ET: "The 'Spirit' and the 'Word' in the Pre-exilic Reforming Prophets"]; Mowinckel, *Die Erkenntnis Gottes bei den alttestamentlichen Propheten.*

12 | The Cultic Myth
Belief and Confession

THE CULTIC MYTH

When that which happens and is reenacted in worship is portrayed in narrative epic form or is sung of in a hymn, myth results. "Why do we do this?" ask the worshippers. The answer is because the deity once in ancient times did this and commanded this activity. Then follows the narrative of his great work. In this way, Australian Aborigine boys at their rites or initiation hear the narratives of the ancient totem fathers and the provider gods of the clan.[1] So also do the young ask at the Jewish Passover and then the father of the household tells of Yahweh's salvific actions at the exodus from Egypt.[2] Real myth is associated with worship. It arose from it, and it expresses that which happens and which once happened in a foundational way—the "salvific activity" which being experienced again is brought to mind.[3] It is not simply that telling about the gods makes myth into myth,[4] but rather that relating narrative about the salvific and experienced foundation of worship and its content. When

---

1. Cf. Söderblom, *Gudstrons Uppkomst*, 109ff.

2. Exod 12:25–27.

3. This perception of what myths actually are I expressed in *Psalmenstudien*, II:24–25, 45–50. Cf. also van der Leeuw, *Phänomenologie*, 346–47, 389ff., and s.v. "Mythus" [ET: *Religion in Essence and Manifestation*, s.v. "myth"]; Widengren, *Religionens Värld*, 134ff.; Buber, *Königtum Gottes*, xi [ET: *Kingship of God*]. [Ed.: Mowinckel, *The Psalms in Israel's Worship*, 1:165–69].

4. This rather superficial explanation is held by Gunkel. See his *Genesis*, 4th ed., xiv [ET: *Genesis*].

we said earlier that the cultic drama presents the myth of the god, that expression was a little inaccurate. It is almost the reverse. The myth expresses in epic form the reality that happens in the cult.

In the explanatory and efficacious words and songs that accompany the cultic actions, the cultic myth is present already in seed. When the Australian Aborigines in their festive totem song depict the eagle, the totem eagle, the primeval eagle, the species of eagles, their flight and power and hunt, the narrative contains some thing of the life of the primeval eagle and its achievements that are once again actualized and become real to the blessing of the totem tribe. We can here speak of embryonic myths, myths in sort of a preliminary stage, or germinal myths. Such myths can, for example, exist in songs that depict them or in an answer to a thoughtful question about what the cultic activity means. But under the influence of imagination and the epic tendencies inherent in man's desire for knowledge, the epic develops a complicated narrative about an original and fundamental "primeval act of salvation." It can deal, for example, with an ancient hero who discovered and first exercised the efficacious rites such as the Australian totem father singers, or with the creation of the world of the entire contemporary community. Needless to say, all kinds of fairytale material can feed into the narrative and give it color and life. So, is it, for example, when creation is perceived as a victorious struggle with a monster of chaos that can represent a spring flood and thereby also the primeval sea, as in Babylonia and in Israel. To the reflective mind, this narrative, which actually deals with that which always occurs in worship, seems to be a narrative of a seminal historic event. The intellect thereby reverses the relationship between worship and myth.

Because it is life itself and the world that are newly created in the cultic festival, the festive myth so often becomes, as has been noted, a creation myth. Thus, we encounter it in Egypt, Babylonia, Assyria, Canaan, and Israel. This creation is "salvation" from all forces that are hostile to life. The myth, therefore, is simultaneously a creation myth and a salvation myth, just as creation is salvation. In Babylonia, the creation epic was the "reading" for the New Year day, that which was to be read. In Israel, too, creation was thought of as a new year, and the New Year Feast as a feast of creation.

The word "myth" says nothing about the extent of how "historical" or not what is narrated is in and of itself. The cultic myth can have an historical foundation. In Israel, the narratives of historical events, such as the exodus from Egypt and the conclusion of a covenant, were associated with the cultic feast and gradually became an essential part of it. There is, then, nothing to hinder our speaking of Christmas or Easter as cultic myths.

But myth does not view these events as simply secular historical events. It sees them from the viewpoint of God's direct actions and reveals the "heavenly" side of history. The historical events have a metaphysical background, just as the "legend" in the book of Job has. The myth and the message gradually receive their final form and receive a share in that holiness that belongs to everything that has to do with worship. The myth that developed from an epic can in turn retroactively influence worship and give it a richer dramatic form. This was probably the case when people in Babylonia acted out the drama of Marduk and the victory over the primeval sea, Tiamat, or when in Egypt they acted out with great vividness and passion, the struggle between Horus and his enemy, Seth.

The testimonies to the experience and reception of the message that worship includes also share in worship's own holiness, as for example in hymns, psalms, and so on. On higher cultural levels, this tradition is established in written form. The "holy" or "canonical" texts and writings of authoritative rank arise in this way.

FAITH

Through the myth, then, the cultic community's faith comes to expression. Faith is the essential moment in the religious and

The Cultic Myth

cultic relationship. It is the response to the divine summons. The summons, the meeting with the holy, revelation, or whatever one may wish to call it, awakens the notion that the deity is present or at least the suspicion that it exists and is real. The divine message in the summons demands that it be accepted and carried out. It demands and rouses obedience. And as soon as it rouses that when it is encountered, it calls also for trust. That which peope believe in, people trusts in. Therefore, the more important moments in the conduct of life and in life attitude derive ultimately from belief.

In the cultic experience and reenactment, that reality which faith has grasped is confirmed.

In the religion of Israel, too, faith was acknowledged as the essential moment in the religious relationship. Israel as a people and as a religious community lived on the faith that came alive on the occasion of a cultic festival and was proclaimed in its rites, myths, and cultic words that Yahweh through certain simultaneous cosmic and historical actions had chosen Israel as his people and had made a covenant with Israel and from now on was and would constantly be Israel's god. The expression of these facts of salvation in the various forms of worship was Israel's confession of faith that became the focal point of its historical tradition.[5] That the covenant presupposed trusting and obedient faith, and that this was a demand from the side of the deity in the covenant, is expressed again and again in the narratives of the people's doubt, dejection, and infidelity during the desert wandering. Note also the Abraham narratives. And that this demand was a permanent one that bound both the people and the individual and that had its practical consequences for the attitude of the people and their leaders in concrete life situations is a central tenet in Isaiah's proclamations.[6]

---

5. Cf. von Rad, *Das Formgeschichtliche Problem der Hexateuchs* [ET: "The Form-Critical Problem of the Hexateuch"].

6. Cf. Mowinckel, *Profeten Jesaia*, 88ff.

In earlier stages in the history of religion, faith was something natural that was not reflected upon. It simply exists and determines concepts, cultic activities, and modes of living. But faith as the bedrock of religion comes sooner or later into apparent conflict with the complicated reality that arises in a more complex culture. In Israel and in Judaism, the conflict arose between the old optimistic living belief that righteousness and blessing or good fortune and, by the same token, bad behavior and misfortune necessarily went together. Then they experienced that the righteous person and the righteous people so often endured want, suffering, or oppression, and that was the basic religious problem. See, for example, the poem of Job. Thus, the individual was led to reflect about the essence and place of belief, and this led then to it being emphasized in contrast to self-confidence and arrogance as, for example, in Isaiah or to dejection and doubt, as in Deutero-Isaiah. In all of the higher religions there appears, therefore, the articulated emphasis on faith—in Buddhism, Christianity, and Islam.

The essence and significance of faith are most clearly seen in the Reformation, where it became the very central point of religion. On the basis of personal experience, the Reformers arrived at the fact that faith most deeply seen and perceived is not humanity's own work. Insofar as it is roused by the proclamation, by the summons from the deity, is it a gift of God that one is to receive in open acceptance and trust.

CONFESSION AND DOCTRINE

As a thinking being, a human has a need to think through and to express in intellectual form the content of myth or the divine proclamation and belief. Thus arose theology, which leads to confessions of faith and doctrine according to specific historical situations and their needs.

Such a confession of belief can be rather short, such as the Israelite confession of Yahweh who had led his people out from Egypt and given them the land, thereby creating deliverance for them (Deut 26:56–59). Another short proclamation is that of the first Christians, "Jesus is Lord" (Rom 10:9) or "Christ died for our sins according to the scriptures" (1 Cor 15:3) The Muslim confession is yet another, "There is no god but Allah, and Mohammed is his prophet." All of these confessions of belief have their origin and their place in the experiences and life of the cult. The Israelite confession was recited at the presentation of the tithe gifts; the Christian confession was recited at the liturgy when the Eucharist "proclaims the Lord's death until he comes" (1 Cor 11:26). The connection between worship and the proclamation of belief is also clear in later Christianity. The so-called "Apostles' Creed," developed from the baptismal candidate's confession at baptism and belongs, even today among us, to the liturgy of the high mass. In the Orthodox Church the Nicene Creed also has its place in the Eucharistic liturgy.

Through a greater and wider theological and philosophical development, the confession becomes a teaching that was gathered around the chief points of the religion, the doctrine. The foundation of the teaching is the message as re-experienced in worship and formed in myth and liturgy. The teaching of the message and its content are kept alive precisely because it plays a vital role in the liturgy. Here it comes to expression in proclamation which can consist of reading the sacred texts as, for example, the reading of the great creation epic about Marduk at the Babylonian New Year's Festival and in the exegesis of them in preaching with doctrine as the norm. Judaism created such a liturgy of the word first, especially in the synagogue. From there, it gave impulses both to Christianity and Islam.

13 | Cultic Actions

EFFICACIOUS ACTIONS

In the introduction it was noted that worship is composed of both actions[1] and words.[2] In reality, they belong indissolubly together; but for the sake of an overview, it can be practical to consider each one separately. Actually, everything is action. Everything that goes on affects something. In cult, something happens all the time. *Dromena* (things which are done) was the ancient Greek term for cultic rites.

That which makes cultic actions what they are and gives them their value as holy actions is that they are efficacious. It is a thought that originally went together with the magical perception of reality: the symbol and the symbolic action are in some mystical way that which they express. An imitation of an actual event has the same reality and effect as the event itself. In worship, that which is to happen or result, is dramatized and happens, as we saw. Cultic actions are such symbolic actions of a dramatic and real kind.

But in worship, in other words in religion, this thought receives another turn and motivation. Cultic actions are efficacious because they are divine. They were originally done by the elevated powers themselves. With such cultic actions they created the world, as we constantly hear in the mythology of ancient peoples, and in worship, the powers repeat this same action constantly.

---

1. Cf. van der Leeuw, *Phänomenologie*, 317ff. [ET: *Religion in Essence and Manifestation*, 339–42].

2. Ibid., 379ff. [ET: ibid., 403–7].

Cultic Actions

The deity is himself present; he exercises his force in actions and works through them. In Israel's cult, it was constantly said that it was Yahweh who had prescribed and instituted the cultic actions. Yahweh's presence gave them their force. That the sacrificial meal took place "before Yahweh" and together with him is that which gave it the power to institute the covenant and to make it continue. When the community carried out worship in the correct way, in the prescribed manner, in the place that Yahweh himself had pointed out, "I will come to you and bless you" (Deut 20:24).

In this way, religion and worship can take over and reshape magical actions. It can obviously happen and has in fact often happened that magical rites, such as that of the rainmaker, which originally had been intended as a purely "rational" action—understood with the primitive perception of rationality—was drawn into the religious sphere and thereby became cultic.[3] But such rites thereby have become something other than they had been. They have become actions which receive their power from their association with the divinity and not from the magician's insight or power. Elijah, to be sure, used old rites of rainmaking in order to evoke rain after the three-year drought. But in the opinion of the narrator of the saga, these worked by reason of the man of God's intense inner prayer to Yahweh. "Water-producing rites" had become symbols.[4]

SACRIFICIAL AND SACRAMENTAL CULTIC ACTIONS

Cultic actions appear to offer a varied and confusing appearance. Since worship is always conservative, it will always contain

---

3. In this pre-religious stage is found, for example, the rain-rites of the Australians; cf. Briem, *På Trons Tröskel*, 163ff., but a certain connection with religion and cult seems to have been in the making. One invokes supernatural powers to give rain and sings efficacious songs which the rainmakers say have been given from higher powers. See ibid., 164–66.

4. This is seen, among other places, in Elijah's behavior in his effort to create rain after the three-year drought (1 Kgs 18:30–45). Here there are remnants of old "magical" rites alongside prayer to Yahweh and where even the prayers themselves contain influences of the ecstatic's supernatural "powers."

very ancient things along with newer ones, diverse actions that stem from various times and that are rooted partially in different mind-sets and motives. The ancient often receive in later times new meanings, often rationalized explanations. They are permeated and reformed by loftier perceptions of the deity that develop. They can also be reduced to inexplicable, unrecognizable vestiges. But certain types of cultic actions will almost always be recognizable.

Cultic actions can be categorized in different ways, such as according to the more special goals which they have. When life is to be created, made secure and increased, two things are important—first, to win and strengthen the good power that nourishes life, to receive a portion in the deity's positive gifts and blessings, and secondly, to remove or ward off everything that is harmful, unclean and sinful. (We shall discuss this in greater detail later.) People have used the term "hierurgic actions" to designate those that are intended to produce holiness, to create, win, increase, transmit (and so forth) "blessing," to win the good will of the deity, or express that the community should share in this. There are also "apotropaic actions" that ward off the encroachment and influence of all evil powers. Finally, there are cathartic or cleansing actions against all manner of impurity and sin. In reality, these move constantly into one another. A means of cleansing is concomitantly a positive supplying of the good forces and a securing of the deity's grace and forgiveness.

One can also divide cultic actions according to their outer form and how they are done. For example, there are mimetic actions that are brought about by imitating in dramatic symbols or "acting out" that which is to happen. Then there are festive parades and processions, dances, various kinds of sacrificing, purification and dedication rites with various sorts of cleansing "material" and so forth. But this, too, becomes a rather schematic way to classify and often fails to delve enough into the essence and meaning of the question. It separates units that belong together.

Cultic Actions

Perhaps the most objective classification is based on the two-sided essence of worship, namely as meeting and fellowship and as mutual action between the deity and the community.

We see that worship consists both of actions and words which, so to speak, go up from below, from the community to God and induce action, and those that descend to the people and mediate God's blessings. We can call the former sacrificial and the latter sacramental.[5]

A gift offering, a prayer for help, and the like are sacrificial cultic acts. Efficacious purifications and other "means of grace," divine assurances, promises, and the like are sacramental. But not even here can distinct boundaries be drawn. One and the same action can contain both aspects. A sacrifice can be perceived both as a gift to the deity and as a means of procuring a share in divine power or as an institution of the deity for the cleansing and the atoning and blessing of the community.[6]

SACRAMENTS AND SACRAMENTALS

Both in the sacraments and in sacrificial actions there is expressed the mutual give and receive relationship between the deity and the community.

In the sacrament, the deity gives something of himself. "The symbol represents and rouses perceptions; the sacrament works," it is said. It changes the situation of the community. After the sacrament, the community becomes something other than it had been: holier, more pure, more humble, more trusting, more given over and inclined to the deity, more filled with the force of life and blessing, or more filled with the spirit of love and fellowship.[7]

---

5. This terminology is used following Quensel, *Homiletik*, 36–37. It is valid not only in the liturgy of the Christian church but in all cults. It ought not to be understood, however, in the rigidly exclusivistic way that Quensel uses it. Cf. Quell, *Kultische Probleme der Psalmen*, 45ff. For "sacrament" and *sacrificium*, cf. Underhill, *Worship*, 42ff.

6. See Pedersen, *Israel*, III–IV:200–375, and s.v. "sacrifice."

7. According to Underhill, *Worship*, 42ff. She speaks especially of the Christian sacrament, but her definition is valid for all belief.

Naturally, Israel's religion also had such sacramentals. The purifications with consecrated water, oil, sacrificial blood, salt, and so forth for the taking away of sickness, impurity, or the guilt of sin (as we shall see in a little detail later). All of these were sacramental actions. Another sacramental action was the sacrificial meal, the offering of celebration "before the face of Yahweh" where, according to the oldest mindset, the sacrificial animal had been "made holy" and was filled with the power of the deity, thereby representing the deity. According to the later and the prevailing thought in the Old Testament, however, the guests at the meal were Yahweh's guests and through table-fellowship came into a sacred covenant with him.

The sacramental moment is present wherever the purpose is to procure and increase power and blessing or to mediate the powers of the deity to the community or individuals. One such cultic action involving the increasing of power would be ritual dance or music. In the ecstasy which they release, power and divinity are experienced. The same is true of "mimetic" or imitative rites. Through rain or sun or light rituals, rain or sun and light are created. The green branches in the festival procession conduct the forces of life and spring into the city and the nation. The war dances illustrate the power and victory of the warriors and the defeat of the enemy, thereby creating victory. Anointing with oil transmits the oil's mysterious power—which indeed everyone can experience, whether it is used as food or as a medicine—to the one who shall be consecrated such as the king. The vegetation rites of fertility worship cause the grain to grow and create fertility for field and folk and flock. All these are cultic rites that the forefathers of the Israelites had experienced and that can be found vestigially later in the Old Testament.

But the meaning of such sacramental rites can change. The thought about the coming of a powerful, personal deity at the festival and his free giving of salvation and gifts gain predominance and press the notion that the rites themselves are effective into

Cultic Actions

the background. Dancing and music, for example, thus became an action honoring Yahweh and received a predominant place in Israel's worship. The green branches became festive decoration and instruments of celebration. The old vegetation rites became symbols that Yahweh had ordained or symbols of the prayer of the community for peace and a good year. The old water pouring ceremony designed to create rain during the Jewish Feast of Tabernacles was similarly changed. In the Talmud, Yahweh says, "Pour water out before me at the festival that the rain of the year can be blessed for you." These actions received more and more a sacrificial stamp.

THE OFFERING

In the sacrificial actions, it is the people who give something of themselves or indeed give themselves to the deity. They play a central role in every religion[8] including that of ancient Israel. This is seen especially in the place of the regulations for sacrifice in the Mosaic law.

The word "sacrificial" is derived from the Latin word *sacrificium*, which means offering. Offering is perhaps the best expression for that movement in common worship that goes from the community to the deity. It may be useful, then, to look more closely at offering in worship. But this shows us again just how schematized the study can be if we draw boundaries that are too distinct between sacramental and sacrificial. The boundaries are fluid, and the thought is complex.

Under the title of sacrifice, a number of effective actions which originally were of many kinds have been gathered in the course of time. Therefore, it is not possible to give a single, all-embracing explanation of the origin of offering. Even in Israel there were various kinds of offerings and different concepts of them at different times. The genuine ancient Israelite offering from nomadic times was the Passover offering. In it, somehow

---

8. Cf. ibid., 47ff.

the whole force and life of the herd were somehow gathered. It represented the whole. Even the life-force of the deity was in it. That there was sacrificing was to say that life was taken so that life could arise. In the common sacrificial meal, the participants shared in the divine life-force. In other places, such as in the Thracian Dionysius cult, we find the thought that the sacrificial animal was the god himself. The sacrificial animal represented both the herd and the community as well as the divine force. Through the sacrificial actions and meal, new life in the new animals which are born in the herd somehow arose, and living power was mediated to the participants. It was a sacramental meal. At the offerings in ancient times in Israel, the sacrificial meal was the most evident. The meal established, renewed and strengthened fellowship and covenant. The deity was present and gave through the ceremonies of dedication, "the blessing of the sacrificial animal," as the priest expressed it. He gave his blessing power in this. Both Yahweh and the community participated in the festival and in the meal. The community were the invited of Yahweh, his guests, and fellowship and covenant both with him and among the community were renewed and strengthened. Yahweh took his portion, which was burned on the altar. The Israelites called such sacrificial offerings "peace offerings" because they created "peace," or actually, wholeness, the harmony of fellowship between the deity and the community and among the community mutually. But the word "peace" contained also the notion of prosperity, good fortune, or well-being. Human sacrifice can probably be explained from the thought of such a "peace establishing" representation. It was not unusual in the ancient Near East, especially as the offering of the first-born who was "consecrated" to the deity. It occurred in Israel as well, probably owing to Canaanite influence. Within the strict Yahwistic cult circles, that was quickly condemned as contrary to Yahwism. The first-born was to be "brought back" with another gift to Yahweh.

 A common viewpoint of the offerings of ancient times is perhaps that they were means of increasing and ensuring bless-

Cultic Actions

ing. When an animal from the herd or a portion of the crop, such as the "first fruits" or the tithe were "consecrated" to Yahweh and thereby were filled by holy power, his blessing, then both the entire herd or the crop of which they were a part were consecrated, blessed, made strong and viable. They also became life-sustaining and strengthening for those who ate them. They thereby shared the blessing that Yahweh had given the animals and the crop.

In the most ancient times, the tribes of Israel, like so many other peoples, thought that the consecration and participation in the sacrificial meals gave the deity himself increased honor, power and blessing.[9] We have traces of such thoughts in Israel. The community "gives Yahweh honor and power" through the cultic psalms. An expression such as to "bless Yahweh" stems from a time when it was believed that even the deity grew on the power which the efficacious, consecrating words contained. Perhaps this was just as the Scandinavians, through their cultic "formula of salvation," "gave gods and goddesses and the fertile soil fortune and praised it for good fortune."[10] But in the worship of the historical Israel (in any case, in the leading spiritual circles), this thought fell to one side. Yahweh needed no such increase of power. He had all power and blessing in himself.

The thought is also ancient and universal that the offering is a gift to the deity. The deity can use such gifts. The offering is his food, and the oldest gifts of offering were edible. Moreover, food is filled with power. Wine gladdens the hearts both of "gods and mortals," as we read in the Old Testament.[11] The odor of the offering was "a pleasing odor" in the nose of Yahweh.[12] Here, as well, people in the oldest times naively believed that the deity's own power and honor were strengthened by food and gifts. This thought gradually became the most strong. The gift of offering

---

9. See Mowinckel, *Psalmenstudien*, V:27ff.

10. See Grønbech, *Vaar Folkeaet*, IV:108.

11. Judg 9:13.

12. Gen 8:21; Lev 26:31; Num 28:2; Lev 1:9, 13, 17; 2:2, 9; and many other places.

was seen as a praising gift of honor to Yahweh that increased his honor by increasing his reputation or his name. But for Israel, honor meant not only what we today see in the word: reputation, respect and so forth. Honor was a spiritual quality, a weightiness (*pondus*), that is what the word *kabod* actually means. Honor was an actual spiritual power. It was an increased will to do great things. To that extent, the old thought survived in the worship of Israel.

But otherwise, it is the viewpoint of honor and the gift of praise which emerged most strongly in the later royal times or in early Judaism. In this way, the first fruits of the field, which originally belonged together with fertility worship and the universally extended pattern of dedicating or preserving the first or the last portion of grain in order to preserve the grain's life and force became in Israel a gift to Yahweh, who permitted them to be given to the priests or the poor. And increasingly the gift received the stamp of a gift of honor and praise. When the viewpoint of gift occurs in its strongest form, it led to the entire sacrificial animal being burned and thereby "sent up" to Yahweh. In Israel, the burnt offering or "holocaust" or the "slaughter" offering and festive offering receded. The daily morning and later also the evening sacrifice in the temple in Jerusalem was a holocaust that was burned entirely on the altar. But then the festive offering received a new meaning. It became an offering of praise to the honor for Yahweh. There arose the simultaneous notion that an attitude toward Yahweh was expressed and that the offering was an external expression of it. A contrite readiness for repentance or an expression of thanks or praise was important. Precisely in the Psalms we find this thought.[13] The psalm—a song, praise, gratitude, and prayer—became itself an offering from the heart.

The thought of the offering's purifying and atoning effect is also ancient. Worship as renewal and a re-experiencing has

---

13. Pss 50:14, 25; 51:18–21; 69:31–32. Cf. Ps 22:27. This is more closely treated in my book *Offersang og sangoffer*, chapters VI, 3e; VII, 4; and VIII, 11. [ET: *The Psalms in Israel's Worship*, 1:195–219, 229–39; 2:18–25].

Cultic Actions

also, as we shall see in some detail later, the task of taking away impurity, sin, and everything that interferes with the blessing and threatens the vitality of life. And the sacred force that, by consecration, is placed in the sacrifice, cleanses away such weakness and impurity. Such a sacrifice the Israelites called a "taking away of sin offering" (in some translations this is often rendered "sin offering"). According to its meaning, we could translate it as "purification offering." This purification and taking away of sin can also be seen and is increasingly seen from a moral viewpoint. The offering atones for sin and takes away its unfortunate consequences. How this is done is the occasion of a variety of explanations. It can be seen in a more or less magical sense: the power in the blood takes impurity away and heals weakness, or the sin and uncleanness, so to speak, are attributed to the sacrificial animal that takes into the desert into the land of uncleanness whatever guilt belonged to the worshipper. Such, anyway, was the case with the "scapegoat."[14] But it can also be seen in such a way that the offering is a humble praise and atonement gift, which inclined Yahweh to be gracious and to forgive, to "take away" or to "cover" the sin and to cleanse impurity. The sacrifice becomes a repentance offering (in some Bible translations this is often rendered as guilt offering). The offering is a "fine" paid to Yahweh, just as one also, in the judiciary, atones for a crime against a person by paying him or her damages. But the weight could also be placed on the attitude that the offering expresses, the contrite readiness to repent and the self-humiliation that it is intended to symbolize.

Offerings can, then, be perceived as means of the purification or atoning that Yahweh instituted so that the community and the individual could have sin atoned and forgiven. In later Judaism, this became the most evident point of view. Among the sacrificial laws in the priestly writing, the purification and guilt offerings are the most important. But the matter could be

---

14. Lev 16:20–22.

perceived in different ways. The blood that is poured on the altar and on the one to be purified could be seen as some mystic material that cleansed or atoned, or more spiritually, the offerings and the rites themselves created goodwill and forgiveness when they were performed in obedience to the instituting laws of Yahweh.

The deepest motive for the offering is the need to give something voluntarily from the direct feeling of indebtedness to the deity. The best shall be given to the deity. Motives can be mixed. One gives in order to receive, in order to win life or strength or honor. But equally strong is the motive to give in order to receive something which one can give again.[15] Or one can give from a direct feeling of gratitude. In Israel, in this way, the offering of gratitude, both what was completely of free will and what one had promised in time of need, became a fixed ritual institution.

The deepest and fullest offering is when a person gives himself or herself. The pious give themselves to the deity as his servants. In Babylonia and Canaan, young girls offered their virginity in service of the fertility goddess. In Israel, Nazirites dedicated themselves to belonging to the deity for various periods of time and placed on themselves all tabus and restrictions that belonged to a "holy" life. The prophet gave himself to the deity to be his spokesman, his tool, the bearer of his message, with whose life and destiny Yahweh could do as he wanted. He led Jeremiah through life-long pain and persecution for the sake of the call,[16] or, as Deutero-Isaiah put it, "the servant of Yahweh" voluntarily offered his life so that "the will of Yahweh shall prosper."[17]

But the offering could harden in form or stiffen in formalism. The richer the offerings, the greater the certainty of God's goodwill and reciprocity. An expensive offering came to be taken as proof of a pious people. Then we meet in Israel's religion a

---

15. See van der Leeuw, *Phänomenologie*, 327ff. [ET: *Religion in Essence and Manifestation*, 350–56.].

16. Jer 1:4–10; 11:23; 12:1–16; 15:1–9, 10–21; 17:9–19; 18:18–23; 20:7–13, 14–18. Cf. Isaiah 6; Ezekiel 4–5; 24:5–13; Hosea 1 and 3.

17. Isa 53:10.

strong reaction against offering, because it had become a substitute for true piety. "I hate and abhor your sacrifices," the prophets often said in the name of Yahweh (e.g., Isa 1:11; Amos 5:21–25). The real sacrifice is the person's inner and spiritual life, the person himself in a spiritual and moral meaning. The composers of the Psalms insisted time and again that the Psalm, the song of praise, was the actual sacrifice "more valuable than oxen with horns and hooves." "Do I eat the flesh of bulls, or drink the blood of goats?" asks Yahweh in the poetry of the Psalms (Ps 50:13). But the song of praise in and of itself is not that which is valuable, but the attitude for which it is an expression. "Sacrifice to God is a broken spirit; a broken and contrite heart you will not despise" (Ps 51:17[18]). The humble attitude which acknowledges sin or the grateful heart which turns itself to God. The prophets introduced a new tone—not sacrifice but social justice! Not sacrifice but true and moral conduct.[18] Most clearly is this expressed in the words of Micah. The people ask:

> With what shall I come before Yahweh,
>   and bow myself before God on high?
> Shall I come before him with burnt offerings,
>   with calves a year old?
> Will Yahweh be pleased with thousands of rams,
>   with ten thousands of rivers of oil?
> Shall I give my firstborn for my transgression,
>   the fruit of my body for the sin of my soul?

And then the prophet answers:

> He has told you, O mortal, what is good;
>   and what does Yahweh require of you
> but to do justice, and to love kindness,
>   and to walk humbly with your God.[19]

---

18. Amos 4:41; 5:4–5, 18–27; Hos 6:6; Isa 1:10–27; Mic 6:6–8; Jeremiah 7; 11:15; Isa 58:1–7; 66:1–4.

19. Mic 6:6–8.

The wholehearted yielding of one's self to God and to the service of the brethren this is the proper sacrifice; the external is only a symbol.

14 | Cultic Words

CULTIC WORDS AND THEIR CONNECTION WITH ACTIONS

Together with cultic actions there also belong cultic words. In a broad sense, one can say that the actual essence of the words is to accompany and express the meaning of that which happens. They are a universal human expression for the spiritual function, for the interplay of thought, word, and act. It is externalized completely from the beginning, both in the play of children and in the rites of the "primitives." "This is the way we do it, this is the way we do it," cry children when they play, in order to delineate the meaning of that which happens and often also to indicate that there is something far more important and deeper than that which is seen merely externally. This means such and such a thing. Symbolic thought or symbolic action must fulfill its actual meaning in that way. When the inhabitant of New Caledonia ignites a fire using the sun, he accompanies his action with the words that both speak of what is meant and are efficacious together with that which is done: "Sun, I do this that you shall burn warmly." The Malayan makes a wax image of his enemy and burns it, but in order for the ritual to be efficacious, he adds the words: "This is not wax that is burning up; rather it is so and so's heart and liver that I am burning up."[1] This sign indicates such and such, says the interpreter of signs or the giver of oracles. When such and such happens, such and such other thing will happen. The oldest rites and cultic actions are most often, like magical praxis,

---

1. According to Nilsson, *Primitive Religion*, 80.

symbolic actions that need to be supplemented by words. One blesses or condemns in the name of the deity because the name itself contains efficacious power.[2]

According to ancient Israelite belief, the spoken word had in itself an efficacious power.[3] This is psychologically correct and realistic and built on experience. But in religion, something more is involved. The most ancient words preserved by tradition are divine words. Both that which should be done and that which should be said in worship is ordained in the beginning taught by the supreme original beings, according to the Australian Aborigines. The same idea appears in various forms everywhere in religions. According to the law of Moses, Yahweh himself ordained the cultic rites as well as the forms of blessing and other words that belong to them. The one thing that most religions know about the origin of such arrangements is that they are very ancient. It has "always" been done in this way. But that means that the "holiness" that they contain has been increased by the holiness that tradition and age give them. If the existence of the world rests on worship, the cultic words are part of the cosmic order. The deity's powerful words created the world, as we hear in Babylonia and even more clearly in Israel. The same word, when it is uttered in worship, is what maintains and renews the world. When Yahweh "sends out his word," that which is borne in the cult by the cultic prophets—the flock who "proclaim the good news"—an end is again brought to all chaos, as we hear in one of the New Year's psalms.[4] The thought about the deity of the cultic words can also take the form that were ordained by the deity himself. When the cultic prophets in ancient Canaan proclaimed their ecstatic words, it was because "the deity had seized them" and spoken through them. In Israel, it was said that "Yahweh's

---

2. On this belief in names, see for example, Heitmuller, *Im Namen Jesu*, 132ff.

3. See Pedersen, *Israel*, I–II:111, 167–68, 200, 235, 242; III–IV:17, 449, 448–54. Cf. also, I–II, s.v. "word"; III–IV, s.v. "word, power of."

4. Ps 68:11–14[12–15].

spirit," his life-giving and creative "spiritual breath," had "gone into them." They spoke efficacious, divine words that created and revealed the future. The same thought is carried over also into the other words of worship. The author of Chronicles, for example, in speaking of the temple singers who set the psalms to music, uses the same word used of prophets when they prophesy. Both the psalms and the rendition of them are "inspired." That cultic words are of divine nature and authority is a thought we meet in Indian, Persian, Greek, and Roman religion. Indeed, we meet it in all religions, including that of Israel. The holy words of worship have power because they are ordained by the deity himself and are spoken "in the name of Yahweh." This is also a fundamental Christian thought. Grundtvig writes of "the divine word" in the liturgy that "creates that which it mentions," that "consecrates the baptism of Jesus and blesses the chalice of Jesus," that "creates good conditions for the Lord's warriors below," and that "makes wine from water and paradise from the desert" and "creates light about the land."[5]

In worship, the power of the action and the word should work together. That which the action says or does in its way, the word should express in its way. It can be said that the word expresses and actualizes the content of the action and the symbol. The totem dances of the Australians illustrate the life and behavior of the totem animal, while the accompanying song describes it. Together, they create prosperity and life for it.

In Israel, we meet this relationship already in the clan or the tribe's old and relatively simple cultic actions where it harmonizes with the whole purpose of worship, namely to create blessing for their own, and to bring damnation upon the enemy. Thus, it was necessary to utter the efficacious word of blessing or damnation so that it reaches its goal and does what was intended.[6] Before Isaac can transmit his blessing and that of the clan to

---

5. *Landstad Revised Hymnal*, #417.

6. For more about that see my book, *Offersang og sangoffer*, chap. XI [ET: *The Psalms in Israel's Worship*, 2:44–52]. See also, *Psalmenstudien* V.

his son, a ritual meal must be arranged. Then he places his hands on his son—this is the action—and blesses him[7]—these are the words. Together, the two transmit the blessing of the clan to the next generation. When the daughter of the clan is to be given in marriage to another house, the clan gathers around her, and gives her the blessing that will make her fruitful and increase the power and honor of her new clan in the days to come. They say:

> May you, our sister, become
>   thousands of myriads;
>   may your offspring gain possession
>   of the gates of their foes.[8]

Certainly this was accomplished both with the laying on of hands and other ritual ceremonies of a cultic nature.

When the tribe is threatened by a powerful enemy or mobilizes for battle, a great festive sacrifice is held. During quite specific ceremonies, which we see depicted in the Balaam sagas, the word of damnation is forged and sent out to break the power of the enemy and place defeat into his soul.[9]

When the priests lift up Yahweh's sacred chest, the ark, in order to carry it ahead in the festival procession or in battle, it means that Yahweh on his throne is placing himself at the head of his hosts. Therefore, they lift the box up with a short song that encourages Yahweh himself to arise:

> Arise, O Yahweh, let your enemies be scattered
>   and your foes flee before you. (Num 10:35)

And when the host gained victory or the festival procession had reached its destination and the box set down, they said: "Return, O Yahweh of the ten thousand thousands of Israel" (Num 10:36b).

On the feast days when the liturgy was over, the high priest gathered its entire content in an act that visibly and audibly was

---

7. Genesis 27.
8. Gen 24:60.
9. Numbers 22–24.

to transmit to the community the blessing that had been gained through it. The high priest extended his hands over the people and recited the well-known "blessing of Aaron," which even today concludes our liturgy: "May Yahweh bless you and keep you," etc.[10] We hear the echo of words that accompanied the cultic ritual cleansing in the seraphic words at Isaiah's consecration as a prophet. The one who performed the purification touched the mouth of the worshipper with one or another cleansing item that was "filled with power." In the vision it is a burning coal from the altar. And then he says:

> Now that this has touched your lips,
> your guilt has departed and your sin is blotted out.[11]

At the trial of a wife who is suspected of infidelity, the priest prepares a drink that is called bitter water. In it a parchment on which has been written an efficacious formula of curse is rinsed out. If she is guilty, this drink will kill her.[12] Here the action and the words are literally together. The action is the offering and the drinking of the bitter water and the words are the written formula. They become an efficacious unity that serves as a ritual "judgment of God" and "ordeal."

This unity of symbol and word occurs in less solemn ritual actions as well. We meet this often in the prophets' efficacious actions.[13] For example when the dying Elisha orders the king to shoot arrows out the window in the direction of Damascus, lays his hands on the king while he is shooting and accompanies every arrow with the words: "Yahweh's arrow of victory, the arrow of victory over Aram." Then he adds the interpretation: "You shall smite the Arameans until it is all over with them."[14]

---

10. Lev 9:22; Num 6:22–27.
11. Isa 6:6–7.
12. Num 5:11–31.
13. See Mowinckel, "Om Nebiisme og Profeti," 342ff.
14. 2 Kgs 13:14–19.

The words are then, so to speak, the accompanying text of the cultic drama. The cultic myth also belongs to the sacred words, as we have heard of the creation epic in Babylonia. But precisely because word and action belong together, the text is often incomplete. Actions must supplement it to make it comprehensible. Therefore, the old cultic dramatic texts very frequently are so fragmentary and disjointed. We usually know very little about the actions that accompanied them. A good example of such an apparently fragmentary cultic text is the Babylonian myth of Ishtar's descent to the underworld.[15] The text says nothing about how she got down there, what she did there or that she came back. All of this could be known from the dramatic actions that once accompanied the text. And songs such as Psalms 24 and 132 give neither context or meaning, if it is impossible to discover the ritual actions that accompany them and filled them out and completed them.

WORDS OF THE DEITY

All the cultic words that we have mentioned above belong to creative cultic action. They are efficacious words. They belong as such to the sacramental dimension of worship. Through them God's own creative power works. They lie on the same line when the cult includes direct words of the deity that are proclaimed to the community as an expression of the deity's will, promise, and help. Both in Babylonia and in Israel there belonged to the regular cultic personnel also a guild of cultic prophets, or reciters of oracles, who partly at the conclusion of the regular festivals and partly as answers to direct questions at times of extraordinary need, such as a day of prayer or petition in need or danger, proclaimed God's gracious response and revealed the divine secrets of the future. Such cultic oracles had their definite place in the festive ritual. At such and such a point, the divine words were to be proclaimed with such and such content. They could also

---

15. See remarks on the literature above, p. 74 n. 10.

appear as an oracle's or temple prophet's interpretation of divine "signs," for example, through the entrails of an animal or other "omens."

Yahweh's assurances of victory, peace, and a good year were part of the ritual at the New Year Festival in Jerusalem. At the enthronement of the king, the temple prophet proclaimed Yahweh's choice and his installation of the new king and promised extraordinary endowments if he kept Yahweh's commandments. On days of petition and prayer, such as before battle, the prophet proclaimed help and salvation. At cleansings of the sick, he promised that the prayer would be heard and health restored and proclaimed the defeat of the evil men and sorcerers who had placed evil in the pious person. Examples and hints of such cultic oracles can be seen frequently in the Psalms.[16]

Both the Psalms and other ritual texts in the Old Testament give us information about another type of such efficacious cultic words, namely the efficacious blessing of the priests on the community, the land, and the nation, as has been discussed above, and similarly efficacious words of curse against the enemies of the nation and all transgressors and sinners whose existence threatened to infect the community with impurity or sinfulness. Such words can also be spontaneous or an established stage in the ritual.[17]

CULTIC MYTH, CULTIC LEGENDS, AND SACRED WRITINGS

In reality, the cultic legend, the narration of the cultic myth, can also be such a divine word of promise. In the reading of the myth about the deity's salvific acts of the past there is "good news" about his constant re-enactment of those great works. In the Canaanite cultic drama, we meet the creative god El and his proclamation of Ba'al's resurrection as the good news. "Heaven shall let down

---

16. See *Psalmenstudien* III.
17. Ibid., V.

rain with oil and the valleys flow with honey for now I know that Alyan Ba'al has come to life and that the master of the world has come lifted up again."[18] Yahweh's self-revelation in the festival has the same form: "I am Yahweh your God, who brought you up out of the land of Egypt" (Psalm 81). We also have in Israel his message through the temple prophet about the blessings that he will now let rain from heaven (Psalm 85).

Originally the proclamation of the message of the deity's coming and salvation took place in and with the presentation of the cultic drama. It contained the message in and together with that which "happened," namely, the good news. When a myth receives its fixed narrative form, as for example in the Babylonian creation epic, sooner or later the epic form itself becomes a sacred text and is seen as canonical with the holiness of the tradition and the cult. Then the reading either replaces the "drama" or becomes a part of it.

So is it also with other religious texts that in one or another way have their origin in worship. "Sacred scripture" becomes the form for the message of the cult. In Israel the proclamation of certain commands of Yahweh were from ancient times part of the New Year Festival, a topic to which we shall return. In Judaism, this became "Yahweh's law to Moses"; it received a fixed and written length and became from the beginning the chief portion of the book of Deuteronomy.[19] Every seventh year it was read aloud at the festival and the custom was later extended to include all of the Pentateuch. From this arose the custom of reading segments of the Law and the Prophets, as well as other parts of the Old Testament in the weekly liturgy of the synagogue. This custom was adopted by the earliest Christian Church. It was natural for the Gospels to be given canonical status as "God's word." They

18. See Hvidberg, *Graad og Latter*, 45 [ET: *Weeping and Laughter*, 54]. Cf. also Ashtarte Yam's message, ibid., 47.

19. Even the lawbook is composed of Deuteronomy 6–30, with 4:4 as the original title. Especially in the last chapters there is a part of secondary development. See Noth, *Überlieferungsgeschichtliche Studien* I [ET: *The Deuteronomistic History*].

were themselves "the message." And very quickly they received first place in the reading of texts in the Church. The Christian kerygma is the factual continuation of this line of thought—"the word of God in the form of human speech."

THE REVELATION OF THE DIVINE WILL

In Israel, we also meet a special form of God's word to the assembly for which there is no parallel in other Near Eastern religions. The strong historical element in Israel's religion, which wholly reshaped the content of the cultic drama, made the renewal of the covenant one of the most prominent thoughts in the New Year and Epiphany festivals. When the temple prophet announced Yahweh's coming in Yahweh's own words he also proclaimed the revelation of his will, the basic commandments that had formed the basis of the covenant and that were now to form the basis of its renewal, as we see in Psalm 81, for example. That means that a strongly ethical and national educational influence plays a role in festive worship. Exhortation is associated with it. All misfortune that the people have encountered is attributed to violation of his commandments. The old traditions narrate that this was already so immediately after the conclusion of the covenant at Sinai. Therefore, the exhortation for this occasion—"today"—admonishes the people to hear Yahweh's voice and not to repeat the disobedience and distrust of the days of the wandering in the desert, but rather to "listen to the voice of Yahweh" and to keep his commandments. The festival's message of promise is predicated on that condition.[20]

At another point in the cultic festival similar thoughts come in, namely in connection with the ancient, universal custom that pilgrims at the temple gate inquire about the requirements for gaining access to the holy place and its blessings. A fixed liturgical procedure developed in the course of time from what was initially a natural rule of conduct. As we can see in Psalm 24,

---

20. Psalms 81; 95; cf. 132. Further treatment in *Psalmenstudien*, II and III.

there was once a fixed step in the festive ritual that the festive procession *must* inquire about conditions of entry and receive an answer from the priests who stand guard at the temple gates. Only those who are pure of heart and have clean hands can be received as "guests on Yahweh's sacred mountain."

In all this we see the "sacramental" element in the words of worship and trace a general line from myth to proclamation, to the place of the promising and hortatory word of God in worship. The line continues to the reading of the Law in the synagogue and to the readings of the gospel and the kerygma in the Christian worship service.

WORDS AS AN EXPRESSION OF THE COMMUNITIES' REACTIONS

But words serve a second purpose in worship. They are to give expression to the emotional reactions of those who experience the cultic drama, paralleling, for example, the singing of the chorus in a Greek drama. Gradually, as the personality of the deity becomes more clearly defined, and the drama depicts the "history" of the deity—his battle and his victory, and possibly his death and resurrection—there is more and more place for an accompanying text. In the Near Eastern Tammuz cultic dramas, for example, psalms of lament for the dead deity play a prominent role,[21] as does the hymn of joy over his resurrection and victory. The deity who comes is praised in hymns. His help is invoked with prayers and laments. The message about what is coming or what deliverance involves is proclaimed by his spokesmen.

---

21. See Witzel, *Tammuz Liturgien und Verwandtes*; cf. also Zimmern, *Babylonische Hymnen und Gebete*, II:10ff.

15 | Prayers and Psalms

CULTIC PRAYER AND ITS FORM

The point with which we concluded the previous chapter shows that words also express the congregation's needs and desires. The most important cultic words are in the last analysis, prayer.[1] It belongs, in distinction to material discussed above, to the clearly sacrificial aspect of worship.

The direct, informal call of prayer to higher powers in moments of need and danger or during an overpowering experience of "the holy"[2] is certainly just as old as humanity's earliest religious life and perhaps older than any cultic formula.[3] But in the old cultures and religions, prayers are above all bound to regular worship. This is true both for honoring and praising the deity who comes and for prayers for help, blessing, and life. Prayer has developed from the very essence and life of religion. It is the genuine expression of fellowship between God and humans that is expressed in worship. It did not "evolve" from anything else. But in worship it comes together with efficacious words and formulas, and under certain circumstances it can degenerate to the point of being regarded as a "magical" formula. On the other hand, in a higher religion and a genuine piety, the old formulas can be lifted up to become prayer. Instead of the more or less self-

---

1. A good sample is gathered and examined by the historico-systematic method by Heiler, *Das Gebet*, 157 [ET: *Prayer*].

2. Cf. Isa 6:5; Luke 5:8.

3. See Heiler, *Das Gebet*, 38ff. [ET: *Prayer*]; van der Leeuw, *Phänomenologie*, 402ff. [ET: *Religion in Essence and Manifestation*, 422–29].

fulfilling words of blessing, for example, prayers occur that the deity may bless. In a sense, this can, under certain circumstances, imply an "evolution" from impersonal formula to prayer toward a personally willing and acting God who is influenced by the words of people but who cannot be bound or compelled by them. The sacred cultic word can occasionally be thought of as "giving power" to the deity.[4] But in Israel's religious life this thought lived on only as remnants of linguistic expression; prayer gave the deity "honor" but also that rested on the humble, believing, and obedient mind that prayed, and the deity himself increased his honor by answering the prayers with great acts of deliverance. Both the song of praise and the prayer for everything the congregation needs in its life finds a fixed place in regular worship.

Since worship is regularity, form, and rhythm, prayers associated with worship also become rhythmic.

Whatever human rhythm is based on, both physiologically and psychologically, and whatever the basis of the need to gather strongly felt words to express strong feelings In rhythmic forms may be, it is a fact that almost everywhere on earth cultic and ritual words—both magic formulas and prayers to personally acting gods—have a tendency to take rhythmic and poetic form.[5] Poetry is the form for the strongest and most comprehensive experiences, and among the strongest and most comprehensive experiences are the religious. For the deity, the most beautiful Is not good enough. Poetry is divine language. Art is always an important aspect of worship."[6] A purely practical consideration often enters the picture. Words that are to be said by many must have a fixed form so that they can be said in rhythm.

---

4. See Ps 29:1 (above, p. 42).
5. Cf. Heiler, *Das Gebet*, 157 [ET: *Prayer*].
6. Cf. Ording, *Estetikk og kristendom*.

Prayers and Psalms

THE CULTIC PSALM, ESPECIALLY IN ISRAEL

This means that the psalm is the natural and proper form for prayer in worship. This is true for prayers praising God as well as prayers of gratitude and petition.

The prayer cast in the poetic form of a psalm, which in itself is proof of inspiration by higher powers,[7] is found in all religions of the ancient Near East: the Indian hymns of offering, the ancient Vedas;[8] the Persian Gathas;[9] the Sumerian, Babylonian, and Assyrian hymns and lamentations;[10] the Egyptian cultic psalms and prayers;[11] the Hittite[12] and Greek cultic lyrics,[13] and so forth. In addition, it is encountered also in the so-called magical songs of the shamans,[14] herbalists, and other "medicine men," and also in the cultic myths of Australian Aborigines.[15]

The cultic ritual prayer, the psalm, as sketched above, is encountered in Israel's liturgy. The Psalms in the Bible are intimately associated with worship, not only in the sense that individual kinds of psalms originally came into being directly in

---

7. Cf. Pss 45:1[2]; 49:3-4[4-5]; 1 Chr 25:1-30 (see above, pp. 112-13). See also the remarks below at p. 128 n. 24.

8. See Lehman in Saussaye, *Lehrbuch*, 2:8ff.; and Konow, 2:12-13; see also Konow in *Illustreret Religionshistorie*, 222ff.; Tuxen in the 2nd ed., 514ff. Examples in translation in Söderblom, *Främande Religionsurkunder*, 2:7ff.

9. Söderblom, *Främande Religionsurkunder*, 2.2:690ff. Lehman in Saussaye, *Lehrbuch*, II³:173ff.; II⁴:207ff.; Christensen in W. Otto, *Kulturgeschichte des Alten Orients*, 3.1:213ff.

10. Many examples in translation are to be found in Jastrow, *Die Religions Babvloniens und Assyriens*, 1:273ff., 393ff.; 2:1ff.; Zimmern, *Babylonische Hymnen und Gebete*; Ungnad, *Die Religion der Babyloniens und Assyrer*, 185ff. Cf. Tallquist in *Illustreret Religionshistorie*, 1st ed., 97ff.

11. See Roeder, *Urkunden zur Religion des alten Aegypten*; Erman, *Die Literatur der Aegypter*, 35ff., 37ff., 83ff.; Lange, *Religiøse Texter fra det gamle Aegypten*.

12. Friedrich, *Aus dem Hethitischen Schrifttum*, 19ff. Cf. Götze in W. Otto, *Kulturgeschichte des Alten Orients*, 3.1:155ff.

13. Examples in Söderblom, *Framande Religionsurkunder*, 3:201ff.

14. Ibid., 3:81-82, 95-96, 101ff., 106ff., 112, 116, 321ff.

15. Cf. Söderblom, *Ur religionens historia*, 99ff.

worship,[16] but also because almost all of the surviving psalms are truly cultic psalms created for worship and used in it.[17] This is true because gradually as the image of God became clearer and more elevated and the personal elements in it became more dominant, and as humanity gradually became more completely convinced of its total dependence on God, and the relationship between God and humans became a personal relationship, prayer in all its forms became a more prominent aspect of worship. This forced the more impersonal and formulaic cultic words in to the background. This is especially true in revealed religion. Israel's religion was based on the awareness of an objective historical revelation of a God who lives and is personal, who wills and acts and establishes goals. He concluded a covenant with this people, and they are in all of their life completely dependent on him. He also demands that the people should totally submit to him in return for what he has done for them. At a very early time—we do not know exactly how early—this conviction set its stamp on the liturgy. We also find early direct evidence of the psalm in the worship of Israel.[18]

If we limited ourselves to the picture of Israel's worship we receive from the cultic laws in the Pentateuch, we could be tempted to believe that it was officially an almost wordless ceremony of sacrifice and ritual. But these laws were not written down in order to give a complete picture of worship and the festivals. They were handed down and formed from special viewpoints. First and foremost they were designed to establish the contributions of the congregation in the worship and rituals for the priests actions in the sacrifice and purification ceremonies

---

16. This is what the work of Gunkel has indicated. See the summary of his view in Gunkel and Begrich, *Einleitung in die Psalmen* [ET: *Introduction to Psalms*].

17. I have indicated this for the most important groups of psalms that occur In my *Psalmenstudien*, I–VI. I give a presentation of the poetry in my *Offersang og sangoffer* [ET: *The Psalms in Israel's Worship*].

18. This is more closely examined in ibid., chap. XVIII, 2. [ET: *The Psalms in Israel's Worship*, 2:146–50].

themselves. But even here there are occasionally words that are to be said or prayers that are to be uttered.[19] And the psalms themselves are an indication of what words meant in the worship of Israel and Judaism.

The songs of the Psalms had their place in the various kinds of worship in Israel at their various stages of development. The hymn expressed praise, respect, trust, and adoration of that just and gracious God who creates, redeems, rules, and "judges"— God who revealed himself both in creation and in the history of the covenantal people and who shows himself ever anew. It has its place both in the festal processions and elsewhere. In the hymn of epiphany, God is praised as "one who comes" and "makes himself known." In the enthronement hymns he is praised as the victorious creator and king who again "has assumed the royal name" and "established the earth" and who has entered upon his reign and established his kingdom and the world against the forces of chaos. His people are established against all their enemies and are blessed with all manner of good.

In need and in danger, in days of repentance and prayer against drought or locusts and other plagues, when enemies threaten land and city, or when Israel's armies have had to yield to the enemy, there resound psalms of supplication and prayer with a depiction of the need and a cry for help and with recitation of everything that can move Yahweh to stir himself and to get involved. Then resounds also the confession of sin and prayer of petition on behalf of the community, or it refers to the "justification" of the people before Yahweh and their rectitude in comparison to enemies and traitors, and it expresses the humble prayer of the people for help and their solid confidence in the God of the Fathers.

When the danger is over and the victory won, the offering of thanksgiving takes place with the psalm of the people that expresses gratitude for the help they received. At the annual fes-

---

19. Num 5:19-23; 6:22-27; Deut 21:7-9; 26:1-10, 12-15; 27:14-26; 30:11-14. See above, pp. 114-15.

tival, the psalm of gratitude for the year's harvest and blessing was sung, as was the prayer for all that the people needed for their life in the coming year. Often in these psalms it is the king who speaks on behalf of the people; his "I" can be changed to the community's "we."

Also for the individual person—originally perhaps for the "great ones" among the people—there was singing of psalms during cultic activities. If a person was struck by sickness and impurity, he brought forward his purification offering. It was then part of the ritual that he—or in reality, probably the temple singer on his behalf—complained about his need in the psalm of personal lament and bade the deity to offer him deliverance or cleansing and the destruction of the evil powers that had fastened evil upon him, or that Yahweh might overlook his sin and let his wrath subside and remove the evil from him.

It often happened under such circumstances or in some other need or necessity that the worshiper made a promise of a thankoffering if his petition were heard. Or someone who had experienced Yahweh's help could on his own initiative bring a free-will offering forward out of gratitude. The psalm of thanksgiving belonged to this festival of thanksgiving with its meal for relatives and friends and the poor of the city. The occasions for such a festival with corresponding psalms could be as many as the dangers and tribulations of life itself. We hear of psalms of thanksgiving from those who had been lost in the desert but had returned safely after a dangerous journey, from prisoners who had escaped from prison, from sick people who had been healed, and from those who had been in danger at sea. All these could be brought together in a common festival of thanksgiving where the expression of thanks on behalf of different groups took place (Psalm 107).

Naturally, many of these different aspects could be bound together. At the annual festival, the psalm depicted how Yahweh had stepped forward to "judge the world" and concluded with the prayer that this might not become a reality (Psalm 82).

Prayers and Psalms

When the psalm is seen as an element in the entire liturgy, it can then be bound together with sacramental moments. It belonged both to the annual festival and to the penitential service of the community or the individual that the priest or the temple prophet expressly answered the prayer with Yahweh's promise of help. The Psalms frequently point to this, and sometimes the psalm texts also contain this promise, "the oracle." Individual texts that have survived in the Psalms are in their totality formed as such divine promises. This is especially true of the promises to the king on the day of his anointing, as in Psalms 2 and 110. But the psalm could also be formed as a dramatic liturgy with changing parts and voices, as for example Psalm 24 and Psalm 132, in which the promise to the king and to the people can also have its place.

The word of blessing could also be part of a psalm (Psalm 115), as could the proclamation of the demands Yahweh imposes on those who would have a share in the blessing of the holy place and worship service (Psalms 15, 24).[20]

SACRAMENTAL ELEMENTS IN THE PSALMS

As a prayer, the psalm belongs to the sacrificial elements of worship.[21] Prayer and psalm are a movement from the person to the deity that greets him when he comes or that expresses humanity's worshipful respect and submission when it draws near to the Holy One or that will incline the deity to come, to listen, to answer and to give. All of the moods of religion are expressed in the psalm. There are cries of suffering from the depths, but there is also "jubilation of my soul before the Lord." There is gratitude for beneficence that has been experienced, and promises of praise

---

20. A presentation of the different types of psalms, their stylistic and content specializations, and their place in the cult is given in the *Einleitung in die Psalmen* [ET: *Introduction to Psalms*] of Gunkel and Begrich which, however, requires many essential corrections. A more detailed examination of this is given in my book *Offersang og sangoffer* [ET: *The Psalms in Israel's Worship*].

21. See above, pp. 103–10.

and of life with God are made. In the psalm the religion's image of God also appears. The facts of salvation are re-experienced. Faith accepts God's promises—"The faith that knows your promises are true," as N. J. Brun writes in his Pentecost psalm.[22]

But, as we have seen, the distinction between the sacrificial and the sacramental is not absolute in the psalms, and it cannot always be made mechanically. Prayer and psalm are inserted into the liturgy that in its totality is not regarded as the work of humans but rather as a divine institution. God comes because he himself wants to and because he wants to show himself as gracious toward his children. This stamp of the divine institution and revelation also marks the prayers and the psalms of the liturgy. In all ancient religions, including Judaism, there is a tendency to view the traditional liturgical psalms as inspired holy words that God himself has given his own to use when invoking him.[23] That poetry is attributed to divine inspiration is an ancient and universal thought in the Near East, one that we find also in Israel,[24] and it is especially true of religious poetry. A special efficacy is attributed to such poems. Such psalms are useful both for driving away evil powers[25] and for pleasing God. This can be dangerously close to allowing prayers and cultic psalms to sink to the level of being regarded as magical formulas that compel both gods and the powers and themselves create that which they express, as happened in the ancient Indian Vedic religion, or that garner "merit" simply by being said from time to time. The most extreme example of such a mechanizing of prayer is the Tibetan prayer-wheel with prayer formulas written on it that can be driven by wind or water power and still serve the same purpose.

---

22. *Lanstad Revised Hymnal*, #439.

23. See, for example, Heiler, *Das Gebet*, 182; cf. 224ff., 353 [ET: *Prayer*].

24. See Mowinckel, *Psalmenstudien*, V:49; and more closely in Mowinckel, *Offersang og sangoffer*, chaps. XVI 3c, XVII 4, XX 5 [ET: *The Psalms in Israel's Worship*, 2:109, 143–45, 187–89].

25. Cf. Mowinckel, "Zwei Beobachtungen," 261ff.

Prayers and Psalms

RITUAL PRAYER AND FREE PRAYER

In the history of religion, liturgical or ritual prayer has played a greater role than free prayer. Even among the prophets in Israel we see very little of the latter apart from cultic occasions and the cultic place.

Basically, this is to be found only in Jeremiah and partially in Amos in any noticeable way.[26] But that free prayer can be present and maintained under no less regulated a prayer system than that of Islam with its fixed times of prayer and prescribed forms, shows that even in Islam the believer can add his own private prayers to the prescribed confession and praise of the *salat*. We see the same thing in Judaism, from Samuel's mother Hannah, who used the homage of the divine festival as an occasion for "pouring out [her] soul before Yahweh" (1 Sam 1:15), to the tax collector in the parable who at the time of prayer could not express anything but "God, be merciful to me, a sinner" (Luke 18:13).

The fixed forms are no hindrance; they are very often a help. Even spontaneous or private prayers can find expression in the prayer forms that are prescribed for the liturgy. Often the liturgy will prove capable of saying that which the individual has on his heart better than his own words. There are many who in the course of time have become increasingly grateful for the help their prayer life has gained by using privately and personally the prayers from our liturgy.

---

26. See Hertzberg, *Prophet und Gott*.

16 | Worship and Morality

TABU: RIGHT ORDER AND CUSTOM IN RELATIONSHIP TO CULT

The relationship between worship and ethics, worship and morality must now be discussed.[1]

As I remarked at the outset, religion has three different external forms, namely cult, myth, and ethics. It would be wrong to assert, however, that morality is derived from cult. Morality has its own independent origin in the spiritual nature of humans as human, both as a social being and an individual. This is true even if one asserts—as Christianity does—that it has its deepest foundation in God's "law." In and with humanity's "image of God" is the possibility for development of such a morality in more or less clear agreement with God's law.

But there is without doubt a close relationship between the cult and morality. And such a relationship is already present in and with the many tabus that involve self-denial, restraint, and regulation. All that is cultic is surrounded by these tabus. Together with these prohibitions and commands exists a strong disciplinary power that builds morality and character and a factor that subordinates the individual to society and the interests of its life and laws. Tabus can be of a morally or culturally irrelevant nature, but they can also be founded in natural and healthy life instincts and develop into moral prohibitions that promote life. It may hardly be doubted that many of Judaism's healthy sexual

---

1. Cf. van der Leeuw, *Phänomenologie*, s.v. "Sittlichkeit." [ET: *Religion in Essence and Manifestation*, s.v. "morality"].

Worship and Morality

moral regulations stem from what were originally sexual tabus whose rational form gradually emerged.

Another important aspect is the relationship between worship and the right order of society. Right order, or "custom," or "law" is anchored in the deity, and the life-renewing power of worship is intended to strengthen and renew the right order of society. In doubtful cases, the deity or the oracle decides, thereby establishing precedents and justice. This was also the case in Israel from the times of Kadesh. There the "spring of justice" (En-mishpat, Gen 14:7) and the "well of the oracle" were central cultic gathering places.

To believers, worship is from the very beginning comprehensive of their society's life, customs, and order—seen and experienced as something that exists and is renewed through union with the sacred powers. In worship, the cosmos is created, the world and life with its laws and its development. The cosmic—and thus social—laws become efficacious through worship.

If the goal of worship is to impart holiness and strength to the life of society, then it follows that it includes the insight or knowledge necessary for society's existence. The rules and forms of worship are wisdom and insight in the most fundamental reality. They are a revelation of the relationships within reality. The old Indian name for the efficacious songs of worship, the Vedas, means knowledge or insight. The Israelites also called certain types of cultic psalms "an efficacious wisdom song," or *maskil*.[2] Closely related to this is the idea that the basic moral laws on which society is based and that are part of the wisdom that higher powers mediated at the beginning are proclaimed to the congregation in worship and set forth as conditions for the fellowship that comprises both powers and people. Among the Aborigines of Australia, such moral regulations of the community are part of the "secrets" that are communicated to boys when through cultic rites they are accepted into adult society.[3]

2. See Mowicnkel, *Psalmenstudien*, IV:5–9.
3. See Söderblom, *Gudstrons Uppkomst*, 141ff.

MORAL THEOLOGY IN ISRAEL'S CULT

In the worship of Israel and Judaism, many points of union for an intimate relationship between cult and ethics gradually emerged. From ancient times on their worship, like that of many other Mediterranean religions, had among its "holy laws" certain conditions for access to the holy place and its blessings. They included both regulations of purity and the like and important social mores. It was important to keep the transgressor and the "ban" that lay on him away from worship and society. The emphasis placed on these conditions of access gradually on certain occasions became a fixed element in the cultic rite itself, especially on the occasion of the great annual festival celebrating the renewal of the covenant. In such psalms as 15 and 24 there is evidence of such rituals.[4]

As mentioned earlier, the presentation of the renewal of the covenant between Yahweh and Israel played an important role in Israel's festival worship. But the presentation of the conditions of the covenant, or Yahweh's laws and justice, was closely associated with the idea of the covenant itself. Every covenant has its customs and laws that express its content and essence. Hence, it was very easy to use worship for inculcating these commands on which the community's welfare was dependent. And this was done in Israel. There is evidence of this in such Psalms as 81 and 95. The former is expressly a New Year Festival psalm; the latter shows the connection between a revelation of the will and the thought of Yahweh's coming as king and his enthronement. Both concepts are characteristic of the New Year Festival.[5] Evidence of this connection is also found in the later command that every

---

4. See Mowinckel, *Psalmenstudien*, V:58–60; Mowinckel, *Le Decalogue*, 141ff; Mowinckel, *Offersang og sangoffer*, chap. XI [ET: *The Psalms in Israel's Worship*, 2:44–52].

5. See Mowinckel, *Psalmenstudien*, II:152ff.; III:38ff.; Mowinckel, *Le Decalogue*, 121ff; *Offersang og sangoffer*, chapter V [ET: *The Psalms in Israel's Worship*, 1:106–92]; see above, pp. 119–20.

Worship and Morality

seventh year at the autumn festival the book of laws would be read aloud for the congregation.[6]

Another interesting thing can be noted here. The conditions of access that are imposed in Psalm 15 are exactly ten in number. And in the psalms mentioned above there stand in the first rank among those that are inculcated those that are also the basis of the Decalogue, or Ten Commandments, above all the commandment to worship only Yahweh. All of the old narratives of the conclusion of the covenant on Sinai include a law of Decalogue in various versions. There is obviously a connection between that law tradition, which we call the Decalogue tradition, and ancient "sacred laws" (*leges sacrae*) about conditions of access to the holy place—so-called "entrance regulations." There is a connection between this tradition and the concept of covenant renewal in festive worship. To put it bluntly, the Decalogue originated in Israel's worship.[7] This is another of the places where Israel's religion has a distinctive element lacking in those of the ancient Near East. If one views the different formulations of the Decalogue from an historical viewpoint and tries to find a common thread in that segment of the history of religion and worship that they represent, the tendency is always toward giving moral demands predominance over purely ritual ones. From the very ancient common customs and presentations, the Yahweh religion created something new and special that gave expression to its own exclusive, monotheistic religion of justice and ethics. That all this comes to expression in worship is exactly what one might expect, so essential is worship for religion.

One of the principal, progressive concepts in Israel's religion is this conviction concerning the intimate union of religion and morality that especially the major prophets proclaimed. Since worship in the final analysis expresses the distinctive nature of the particular religion in question, the worship of Israel and Judaism must have been more or less characterized by this re-

---

6. Deut 31:9–13. See above, pp. 119–20.
7. Cf. Mowinckel, *Le Decalogue*, 114–62.

lationship, even though the interest in moral commands among the prophets often took the form of a polemic against the externalized ritualism in the cult. They were themselves stamped by the moral thought patterns that were bound to worship, which they in turn influenced.

17 | Impurity, Sin, and Purification

PURITY AND IMPURITY

Our description of worship would lack an essential element if we did not say something about impurity and sin. Impurity[1] goes together with evil, harmful power and the evil powers in existence. As long as man is right—that is to say normal, healthy, and blessed—he is also pure (Hebrew *tahor*), a notion that occurs in all religions. In and of itself this has nothing to do with the modern rational concept of being cleansed or free of dirt, even though it developed in analogy with the natural notion of washing oneself and derives its conceptual elements from that notion. A person is unclean when he is no longer "right," when power departs from him. When a person becomes sick, when a sword becomes dull, or cattle weak, or plants sick, when a woman is weak by reason of childbirth or menstrual difficulties, when cows abort their calves, or when nature withers away in the fall, so are all of these then "unclean." Their proper power has abandoned them and something strange—a harmful or an evil power or a curse—has come upon them.

Many things can bring this about. Natural wear and tear, as we would call it, is one common cause. Experience certainly teaches humans, as we have seen, that power in the garden or in fruit trees must be renewed at certain intervals. It can be that the person or the thing has come upon something in itself strange or unclean, for example, a corpse or an "unclean" animal such as

---

1. Cf. van der Leeuw, *Phänomenologie*, 320ff. [ET: *Religion in Essence and Manifestation*, 343–49]; and Pedersen, *Israel*, I–II:337.

a snake or a lizard. The weakness and uncleanliness can then be blamed on demons, sorcery, or curses. The Israelites were also aware of such unclean harmful things (*debar beliya'al*).[2] These could be unclean animals, unclean places, human excrement, corpses, female bleeding due to childbirth, menstruation, the loss of semen among men, and so forth.[3]

The unclean has to deal with the curse and the demonic. When the forces of death and chaos hold the ground and the world in their grasp each time the year draws to a close, this means that the world and the land have become worn out, not right, not normal, and not clean. Impurity and sin upset the fixed order of nature.[4] This means not only that God punishes the sinner with disintegration, but also that there is an inner cosmic context in this action.

> How long will the land mourn,
>   and the grass of every field wither?
> For the wickedness of those who live in it . . . (Jer 12:4)

Evil and sin are themselves one side of impurity, as we shall discuss shortly, and this impurity is so contagious that the land itself becomes unclean and "belches out the one who dwells in it."[5]

That which is "foreign" also is usually associated with being unclean, and in worship that which is new. Thus, for the Israelites the camel was an unclean animal, since their semi-nomadic ancestors were donkey and "small cattle" nomads, not Bedouins. The camel was first tamed and taken into general use in the

---

2. Ps 41:8[9].

3. Unclean animals, Lev 11:1–47; Deuteronomy 14; unclean places, Amos 7:17; human excrement, Ezek 4:12–14; Deut 23:13; similarly Jer 16:5–8; Deut 16:14; Hos 9:4; corpses, Num 19:11; Ezek 43:7–9; human bones, 1 Kgs 13:2; 2 Kgs 23:14, 16, 20; impurities of birth, Leviticus 12; leprosy, Leviticus 13–14; Num 14:10–12; bodily discharges, Lev 15:1–33. See Stade, *Biblische Theologie des Alten Testament*, I:138ff.

4. Hos 4:3; Jer 3:3; 12:4.

5. Jer 2:7; 3:2, 9; 2 Sam 21:3; Lev 18:28; 19:29; 20:22; cf. Pedersen, *Israel*, I–II:358ff.

Impurity, Sin, and Purification

course of the thirteenth century BCE or a little earlier.[6] Clean animals were the domesticated animals of Palestinian agriculture. Everything that had to do with other, "foreign" gods and their worship, therefore, was especially unclean. The more exclusive a religion becomes, the stronger is its need to make its practices unique. To the ancient Semites, including the Hebrews, as mentioned above, the deceased ancestors were especially "holy," representatives of the "power," and objects of veneration. Even at the time of David the dead were commonly buried in the home.[7] In historical Israel, opposition to Canaan's dying and rising fertility gods made everything associated with death and the dead, especially worship of the dead in any form, increasingly unclean.[8] Even an age that attributed to Yahweh power over heaven and earth and the underworld asserted that he had nothing to do with the realm of death, *Sheol*. There he did no miracles; the dead were snatched out of his hand.[9] The Old Testament uses the ancient Semitic expression for the divine powers, "the holy ones," as a rule for those divine beings with which the right-minded Israelite was not permitted to have anything to do.[10]

This opposition to that which was foreign gave impurity a special tone and gradually a new content. If the strange is unclean, then the expelled is no less so. The one expelled is one who has violated the order, laws, and mores approved by society. The transgressor is unclean. Yahweh's laws, rules, and regulations are clean.[11] They included society's mores and order, i.e., morality, from Kadesh and the time of Moses.

6. See Albright, *Archaeology and the Religion of Israel*, 100.

7. 1 Sam 25:1; 28:3; 1 Kgs 2:34.

8. Deut 26:14; Hos 9:4.

9. Pss 6:7[8]; 30:10; 88:10–12[11–13]; Isa 38:18–19; Sir 17:27; Bar 2:17–18; cf. Ps 115:16–17.

10. Pss 16:3; 89:5, 7[6, 8]; Hos 11:12; and other places. Other things that are unclean or cause uncleanliness are tattooing, transvestitism (a reaction against cultic immorality and the female and male prostitutes), and so forth. See Stade, *Biblische Theologie des Alten Testament*, 1:145ff.

11. Ps 19:8–9[9–10].

CLEANSING FROM IMPURITY

That which has become unclean must be "cleansed," that is to say, the evil power must be taken away or driven out and a new "clean" power must flow into the particular person or thing again. Cleansing therefore has both a positive and a negative aspect. The most important means of cleansing is based on natural experience—washing with water. That the thought here is not modern and hygienic can be seen, for example, from the custom of the ancient Persians that something should be "purified" with the urine of cattle. Other efficacious means of cleansing are fire, salt, oil, blood and temporarily refraining from such natural things as sleep or sexual intercourse. All these also occurred in ancient Israel.[12] But something positive is also involved In all of this. All these have "clean" power in themselves that goes into the person or thing to be cleansed. Water, oil, salt and fire are "filled with power." The infusion of power makes the person or the thing "right," "clean," and healthy again. This is especially true of blood and explains the increasing weight that in the cultic law of Israel was put on blood in the "purification offering" ("sin offering"). Blood cleanses. In the parlance of comparative religions, it is full of *mana*. Restraint or asceticism are also considered valid in all ancient religions for increasing power.[13] In Israel, those who were especially endowed with power, the Nazirites, maintained their power in so far as they restrained from things which were tabu for them: wine, handling corpses, cutting their hair, and so forth.[14]

All this has in itself something to do with the extraordinary that lies very close to the religious sphere. The holy is in itself

---

12. Cleansing agents: water, Lev 15:13; Num 8:7; 2 Kgs 5:10; fire, Isa 6:6–7; salt, 2 Kgs 2:20–21; blood, Lev 14:5; oil, Lev 14:17; ashes from the sacrificial animal, Num 19:9–10; dust from the temple floor, Num 15:17; the washing of clothes, Exod 19:10, 14; restraint from intercourse, Exod 19:15; 1 Sam 21:5. Cf. Stade, op. cit., 1:142ff.

13. Cf. Schjelderup, *Die Askese*; van der Leeuw, *Phänomenologie*, 433ff. [ET: *Religion in Essence and Manifestation*, 455–58].

14. Numbers 6; Judg 13:5, 14; 14:16, 19; Amos 2:12. The archetype of the Nazirite is Samson, who is "filled with power."

pure. Sacred power and everything that has to do with it are powerful means of purification—in the right hands and when used in the right way. It is understandable that such purification receives a ritual stamp and that worship has incorporated many of them. In Israel we find all of them as cultic customs. The priest is consecrated and purified; he becomes even more pure and powerful than an ordinary person by those same means that are used for cleansing—oil, blood and so forth.[15]

SIN, ATONEMENT, AND RECONCILIATION

If the unclean stands in opposition to the clean then it stands in stronger opposition to the holy. To be sure, *tabu* and the dangerous aspect of the sacred can sometimes be stressed so strongly that in practice the holy seems unclean to ordinary people. It transmits a quality of holiness to them that must not be profaned by coming into contact with the everyday (the "profane") and there by becoming dangerous. Hence, the Jews, for example, say of their holy writings that they "soil the hands"—that is to say, it is necessary to wash the holiness off one's self after one had touched them. But after its kind the holy stands in still a sharper opposition to the unclean than to the profane. Everything that is holy is intrinsically pure, but not everything that is pure is holy. But the aspect of purity in the holy can be so stressed that the pure comes to mean the same thing as holy. In the Persian religion, the two concepts are nearly identical, and in the Babylonian language "pure" (*ellu*) is the ordinary word for that which in Hebrew is called "holy" (*qadosh*).

The unclean is therefore opposed to everything that has to do with religion and worship. Everything that Yahweh had to do with was both pure and holy. Yahweh brooked no impurity. "Your eyes are too pure to behold evil" (Hab 1:13). "No impure eye can look on your holiness." The impure receives a special tone

---

15. Exod 29:20.

when it is juxtaposed with the Holy. The deity loathes that which is impure.

When that which is impure and transgressing (evil) is seen in relation to the deity, it appears to the consciousness as sin.[16] Everything that Yahweh hates is impure, as is everything that is done against his will. And all such is sin. The words for sin in various languages can have many etymological basic meanings, but that which is common to all of them is a depiction of opposition to God's essence and will. Sin has become the typical religious word for that which is wrong, for that which is "evil in the eyes of the Yahweh," that which separates from God. One of the great steps forward in religion, in the history of revelation, was made when this concept was widened to include not only ritual and cultic use and tabus, but also violations of that which is "right," i.e., the community's ethos and morality, and an incorrect, evil, or impure mind—was formed by not only what goes into person but what comes out from the heart. This step forward in Israel was especially represented by the prophets and reaches its perfection in Jesus.

In view of the connection between impurity and sin and ancient peoples' whole concrete way of thinking and conceiving things, it is understandable that their concepts of sin often had a material stamp. Impurity and sin are depicted as something material that can be poured into or placed on a person. It is an evil power, a cursedness, which bears its evil consequences within itself, which produces weakness and impurity and sickness and bad fortune, which eats away at the soul, which makes it weak and crooked, and finally brings death. It infects the whole clan if it is not rooted out and radically purified. With the passage of time there emerges the thought of sin's consequences as the deity's punishment for disobedience and transgression. But there

---

16. For Israel's perception of sin, see, for example, Stade, *Biblische Theologie des Alten Testament*, I, s.v. "Sünde"; Pedersen, *Israel*, I–II:411–52; III–IV:359–65, 458–61, 620. For the universal religious phenomenon, see van der Leeuw, *Phänomenologie*, 431ff. [ET: *Religion in Essence and Manifestation*, 454–55].

Impurity, Sin, and Purification

is no sharp boundary between the notion of "fruit of sin" and "punishment," and between "purification" and "atoning."

Here it is, then, that worship appears. Rites, ceremonies, and words intended to "cleanse," "take away," "wash away," and "blot out" sin, and atone for it, have an important place in all worship.[17] All such means are first used for cleansing. But something else gets involved, for sin is an offense against a personal God. God's anger must be appeased and atoned for; humans and God must be reconciled with one another. Here there arises first the offering, the gift, penance, and prayer. But the old ideas about cleansing and taking away live on. In Israel, we see, therefore, that the ancient purification offering in the passage of time took on increased significance, and that one attributed a purification power to the sacrificial blood, either when it was smeared on the sinner to be purified or poured out on the altar before Yahweh.[18] The need for such purification from sin became widespread. The laws enumerate a number of sins, both conscious and unconscious, which must be atoned for with a purification offering (sin offering). Both the individual violator and, at certain intervals, the entire land and people, must be purification from sin, or "de-sinned" as the Hebrew expression actually means. The highpoint is reached when these rites take place on the Day of Atonement, where both temple and high priest are purified by all manner of "de-sinning" offerings and ceremonies.[19]

This goes back to an older custom that we also know from Babylonia: at the great annual festival both the temple and the king were purified, de-sinned, and consecrated anew, and the king was once again installed in his position as the mediator

---

17. Cf. Stade, *Biblische Theologie des Alten Testament*, 1:3, 203, 310, 315–16, and s.v. "Sunde"; Stade-Bertholet, *Biblische Theologie des Alten Testament*, 2:34–35, and s.v. "Sunde" and "Vergebung"; Pedersen, *Israel*, III–IV:364–65.

18. All of the sacrificial laws in the form they were given in the "priestly writings" (relatively the latest of the pentateuchal sources), witness to this. See Lev 4:5; 6:17—7:6.

19. Leviticus 16.

between the gods and the people.[20] When Yahweh arrived at the annual festival, it meant that he defeated and rooted out all sources of impurity, all sins, everything that is demonic, and "heals the sin of his people." This means cleansing from everything that has made the land and people unclean during the time that has passed and has spoiled power and blessing. At the end of the year nature is dead as a consequence of sin and impurity. All this impurity must be cleansed, and a large number of cultic rites are aimed at accomplishing this. True enough, Yahweh crushes and sweeps away the source of impurity. But all of its byproducts must be taken away. Therefore, it is completely logical that before the day of epiphany and the day of enthronement there must be a considerable ritual cleansing of the king, people, temple, priesthood, city, and land. Symbolically, all of this is gathered together in the ritual of the scapegoat, on which all the sin and impurity of the people are laid. It is then driven out into the desert, to the demons, where impurity and the curse are at home.[21] It is this aspect of New Year worship that later became an independent Day of Atonement, five days before the New Year Festival.

Here, then, the old magical thoughts continue to live, as often just below the surface. But the gracious will of the deity can also be emphasized as the decisive factor. It has pleased him to arrange all of these sacraments in order to free his people from their sins. This is the chief viewpoint in Judaism.

THE ACKNOWLEDGMENT OF SIN AND PRAYER FOR HEALING

But here emerges something even more important. The sinner must humble himself and do penance before God. And to this there belongs not only the external penitential rites of "sackcloth and ashes," fasting, and different types of restraint, such as refraining from sexual intercourse, but similarly prayer in pre-

20. Cf. Pallis, *The Babylonian Akitu Festival*; Frankfort, *Kingship and the Gods*, 313ff.

21. Cf. Zech 5:5–11.

Impurity, Sin, and Purification

scribed forms for the deity's forgiveness and freedom from the evil consequences of sin. Such cultic prayers are the lamenting and penitential psalms that take such a prominent place among the biblical psalms.[22] To the cleansing and offering that was ordained in Jerusalem for the sinner, either he, or the priest on his behalf, had to recite such a psalm of lament before Yahweh. This was also the case both in Babylonia-Assyria and Egypt. A prominent place among these psalms of prayer was devoted to the acknowledgment of sin. It meant both that the sinner should give Yahweh justice (or honor) by acknowledging that Yahweh is just, and that misfortune has struck the sinner justly. In doing so, the sinner hoped to "appease" Yahweh. But the acknowledgment responds also to an immediately spiritual need and an inner-religious necessity. Nor did the ancient Israelite doubt that Yahweh knew his sins beforehand and with righteousness has "found them out." He also knew the immediate and primary inner compulsion that is expressed in our hymnal:

> I stand before God who knows everything
> And cast my eye downward in shame.

The Israelite psalmist also experienced that:

> While I kept silence, my body wasted away
>   through my groaning all day long.
> For day and night your hand was heavy upon me;
>   my strength was dried up as by the heat of summer.
> Then I acknowledged my sin to you,
>   and I did not hide my iniquity;
> I said, "I will confess my transgressions to Yahweh,"
>   and you forgave the guilt of my sin.[23]

Even though misfortune has pricked his conscience and compelled him to see and acknowledge his sin, something that

---

22. See Gunkel and Begreich, *Einleitung in die Psalmen*, 117ff., 172ff. [ET: *Introduction to the Psalms*, 82–98, 114ff.]; Mowinckel, *Offersang og sangoffer*, chaps. VI–VIII [ET: *The Psalms in Israel's Worship*, 1:193–246; 2:1–25].

23. Ps 32:3–5.

still happens to the Christian today one can nevertheless exclaim with all one's heart:

> Happy are those whose transgression is forgiven,
>   whose sin is covered.
> Happy are those to whom Yahweh imputes no iniquity,
>   and in whose spirit there is no deceit. (Ps 32:1–2)

Therefore, we see that precisely in these same cultic psalms the thought comes increasingly to the fore that the decisive thing that Yahweh will have is not the offering and the atonement rituals in themselves, but the psalms together with prayer and acknowledgment of sin, gratitude, and praise, just as the wisdom psalms often assert that obedience is better than sacrifice. A similar tendency is encountered also in Babylonian and Egyptian psalms, and to a certain degree the high value that the temple psalmists and singers placed on their part of the divine liturgy lies behind all this. But this is not the deepest motif. That emerges in the thought that we also find in Israel's cultic psalms and that according to all the evidence was unique to the religion of Israel—namely that the psalm is an expression for the humble and repentant or grateful and obedient *mindset* and that the acknowledgment of sin and the psalm has its value in the eyes of God.[24]

But this does not differ in principle from worship as such. It is the psalm's acknowledgment of sin and expression of gratitude "in the assembly of the community, here in Jerusalem, in the site of your people" that is being thought about all the time. It is as a member of the community, often on behalf of the community and in the public liturgy that the confession of sin by the individual sinner and his penitential prayer has its place. The psalms and temple prayers also acknowledge Israel's sins and pray for forgiveness of sin for the whole nation or the community. They are an expression of the life-encompassing experience of worship

---

24. Psalms 40; 51; and 69 are especially characteristic examples. See above, p. 106 n. 13.

as a meeting with God. They express the power and renewal that the cult should give or in fact gave.

FORGIVENESS OF SIN

The promise of the forgiveness of sin on behalf of the deity, therefore, has its place in the order of worship. The actual content of the "de-sinning" and purification rituals becomes the assurance of the forgiveness of sin that it contains and gradually becomes a symbolic expression for such forgiveness. Precisely the psalms of lament and thanksgiving point often to this divine promise through the priest or temple prophet who was obviously part of the ritual for sin offering and for purifying actions.[25] When the poet in Psalm 32, which we quoted above, says "and you forgave the guilt of my sin," he was pointing to the purification ceremonies and the promise of the forgiveness of sin, both of which were confirmed in the healing for which he sang a song of thanksgiving on the occasion of the thankoffering. The same is the case in the lament of Psalm 6 where one prays to Yahweh not to punish him in his anger, but to free him from the sorcerers who have placed evil on him and threatened his life. In the psalm's last portion, the anticipating certitude about the prayer being heard where he turns to his enemies with a triumphant "Depart from me!" he also says:

> Yahweh has heard the sound of my weeping.
> Yahweh has heard my supplication;
> Yahweh accepts my prayer. (Ps 6:8b–9[9b–10])

Between the occurrence of these two portions of the Psalms, something has obviously happened, namely the promise about the forgiveness of sin a promise of prayers being heard and help given. That is the source of the triumphant certainty. This is a very ancient cultic tradition, but also something that renews it-

---

25. Cf. Gunkel and Begrich, *Einleitung in die Psalmen*, 243ff. [ET: *Introduction to Psalms*]; Mowinckel, *Psalmenstudien*, III:101–5; Mowinckel, *Offersang og sangoffer*, chap. XII, 2 [ET: *The Psalms in Israel's Worship*, 2:58–61].

self on the basis of the very essence of worship and religion. This happens when the confession in our liturgy and the acknowledgment of sin are followed by the priest's promise: "on God's behalf and authorized by his holy power" of "all forgiveness of all of your sins in the name of the Father and of the Son and of the Holy Spirit" and when this entire portion of the liturgy concludes with the hymn of gratitude for the forgiveness of sin.[26]

---

26. For the general meaning of forgiveness of sin in religious "phenomenology" and history, see van der Leeuw, *Phänomenologie*, 512ff. [ET: *Religion in Essence and Manifestation*, 536–37].

18 | The Problem of the Origin of Religion

INTEREST IN THE QUESTION

Since modern study of religion began, it has constantly been occupied with the question about the origin of religion. This is not simply because modern scholarship in religion is historically oriented, but also is due to the aspect of the personal, existential interest that religion has for all who get involved in it, even if this interest often includes a negative aspect. In religion, one cannot avoid the question of its truth. The total demand of religion and its essence as a message of absolute character make it unavoidable. And here, then, arises the question of its origin.

The phenomenology of religion also encounters this question, even if in the strictest sense it wishes to be only descriptive and narrate and explain the phenomena that are actually found in the world of religion. We have previously encountered this many times with regard to the relationships between religion, worship, and magic. We saw that the worship resulted from religion, not vice versa. And we also saw that religion and magic are two essentially different phenomena that cannot be derived from one another, even if they constantly touch on one another in many respects.

EXPLANATIONS OF THE ORIGIN OF RELIGION AND THEIR INADEQUACY

When, where, and how religion came into existence is something that no man knows. The tools of scholarship are of no help in answering that question.

Religion and Cult

We have seen above that religion cannot be derived from magic. They are two different things. Nor does religion derive from the magical or pre-logical view of reality; this at best provides only the background for religion's first occurrence and material for its formation in worship and concepts. It cannot, therefore, either be derived from animism or "belief in *mana*." On the contrary, religion absorbs these notions into itself. Everything in which power or holiness reveals itself, such as things of nature, fetishes, totem or other ancestors, and so forth, is drawn into the religious sphere and "made into gods" or more precisely, regarded and experienced as occurrences of the godlike and the deity.

None of this explains the origin of religion or belief in God. Religion is already there and sanctifies all these things and sees gods or God in them. It is not speculative or practical preoccupation with such essences that has brought religion into existence.

In the strictest sense, we have no grounds for asserting that such concepts as belief in *mana* or belief in the soul are older than religion. The first emergence of religious experience may well be older than the concepts of power, the soul, and so forth.

HYPOTHESES ABOUT THE HIGH GODS

In recent times, it has occasionally been asserted that religion originated in belief in the so-called high gods or superior gods.[1] This involves the notion that one or several are superior to all other elevated essences, which are associated with sky or heaven and are thought of as creators and producers of the world, humans, and all other living beings, as well as the development of culture and the social and religious order. As a rule, they are

---

1. The foremost representatives of this view are Lang, *The Making of Religion*; and W. Schmidt, *Der Ursprung der Gottesidee* I. Cf. also Widengren, *Hochgottglaube im alten Iran*; Widengren, *Religionens Värld*, 57ff.; Birkeli, *Religlonshistorie*, 1:217ff. For a criticism of this exaggeration and oversimplification, see Mowinckel, Review of Geo Widengren, *Religionens Värld*, 187–92; Frankfort, *Kingship and the Gods*, 355 n. 13.

The Problem of the Origin of Religion

perceived as distant and elevated over humanity's worship and prayer.

The theory of the high gods as the original ones can be combined with orthodox church teaching to form a theory of a kind of primeval monotheism, of which the concrete religions are depraved descendants.[2] It is also occasionally asserted that many of the concrete or proximate divine forms are "spin-offs" of the "high god," independent beings derived from one aspect of his essence and activity. It is true enough that such "spin-offs" occur. A god's characteristics and actions can somehow be made independent and perceived as personal essences (hypostases).[3] One god can, so to speak, be divided into many.[4] But this is a relatively rare phenomenon. And in answer to the whole theory, it must be said that even if belief in the high gods really is the oldest known form of religion, this fails to explain the origin of religion. How, then, did this belief in the high gods originate?

But even the belief in high gods is not something universal as some scholars would have it. Belief in such distant generative gods is found especially among the Australian Aborigines and African tribes. The transition between them and the so-called "culture heroes," the primitive ancestors and wise men of primeval times—who discovered the various crafts and arts and who founded the cultic order and rites and laws—is fluid. But scholars have often established here an artificial type, one that on closer examination is seen to include many highly divergent kinds of gods in Itself. There is an essential difference between the generative divine beings of the Australians and the Africans—divine beings that in primeval time called forth the world, culture, and worship, and that since then have lived transcendent, having nothing more to do with the world and with people,[5] and, for

---

2. It was especially Schmidt (*Der Ursprung der Gottesidee*) who proposed this theory.

3. Cf. Mowinckel, "Hypostasen."

4. Bertholet, *Götterspaltung und Göttervereinungen*.

5. Söderblom, *Gudstrons Uppkomst*, 109ff.

example, "The Supreme God" of the Babylonians and Egyptians who most often is one of many originally uniform and all-embracing cultic gods, who because of political circumstances—the centralized state and so forth—and theologians' reflection has become the supreme god, the divine king and the divine father. One only muddies the waters by defining the concept "high gods" so widely that it embraces whatever god happens to be number one in the hierarchy or has something to do with the sky or with fertility or with destiny. The most appropriate thing to do would be to adhere to the limits set by the first students of this type, Andrew Lang, Nathan Söderblom, and others, and define the higher gods as source-essences. They are those now remote and elevated beings that in their time brought forth the world, culture, and the arrangements of human life and who sometimes still intrude to maintain the laws of life. They stand behind whatever is and happens and have rather often a stamp of destiny gods. They are "fate." But they are sometimes a summary of all power and all powers in a large common power, such as the Indian Wakanda or Manitu.

Or it could be that belief in the primitive ancestors and belief in the totem have contributed to the origin of several higher gods. This is essentially what van der Leeuw means when he calls them "the power in the background," but they could just as easily be called gods in the background. But essential for them is that they can be attributed just as much to an intellectual need—a drive to an all-embracing explanation of the world— as to a practical religious need or a magical need for their existence. They are the explanation for that which is, and as such they are more cosmological than religious. They are more philosophical, in the more primitive meaning of the word, than they are religious gods. But they can also have their cult, and prayers can be directed to them, precisely because they are the power behind the powers. Especially where such a higher god is associated with the sky, he can have practical significance as the origin of the sun, light, thunder, and the moon, or as the giver of rain and fertility. Higher gods of this kind are the Babylonian Anu, the Canaanite El, and the Chinese Shang Ti/T'ien. All of these are sky gods. On the other hand it is complete misunderstanding when some in most recent times have wished to perceive the Israelite Yahweh as such a background god—even when they glossed this over by calling him "the West Semitic high god, sky god, and fertility god."

There is one correct aspect in the modern theories about these superior gods as the source of belief in God, however, namely that religion in the sense of belief in and relationship to personal divine beings is independent in relation both to the magical worldview and to magic as praxis.

But no explanation of the source of religion itself is provided by these "philosophical" essences. It is simply impossible to explain the derivation of religion as a practical relationship, a response or a total reaction to the experience of the sacred on the basis of any kind of concept of God. It is true that a concept of God is central in religion and that all of its other concepts and customs are more or less consciously determined by and organized from it. But the concept of gods or a god are derived from religion, not vice versa. How this can be understood more exactly is something that we shall come back to shortly. It is experience, in the broadest sense of the word, that creates the concept. It is the summons that calls forth the response. It is religion that has taken possession of the high gods as well as power and drawn them into its sphere. This is clearly seen among the Australian Aborigines. Their highest beings stand with one foot in the world of cult and religion, so to speak, and in certain circumstances they receive prayers and rites that are directed to them.[6] It is religion that has placed its hand on the concepts of the totem and that gives the totem ancestors the stamp of being gods. Among the Aborigines, the gods of origin and the totem fathers are very closely associated. It is religion that has "sanctified" power, and it

---

6. See Briem, *På Trons Troskel*. 242. Cf. above, p. 36 n. 10 and p. 99 n. 3.

is also religion that has turned many magical arrangements into cultic rites.

RELIGION AS SOMETHING UNIVERSAL

Precisely in worship something essential about religion comes to light, namely its character as a response to a call, a reaction to an experience. But we can add something. It is a total reaction on the part of humanity that determines his entire attitude toward life. That which happens when religion comes into existence for a person is that across his usual perceptions of the world, whether that of primitive perceptions of might, or of the most highly developed spiritual life, there is met something that stands as a supra-worldly reality, an experience of a holy and compelling character. And this reality humanity meets as a Thou in the presence of its I, an overpowering Thou, and humanity recognizes its dependence on this Thou, and its distance from the Thou, and its attraction to it. It sees that one as a Thou who bends down and lifts up, who takes away and gives, who binds the observer to itself and thereby sets him free, who causes fear and thereby drives all other fear away, who gives love and awakens a responding love. Thus humanity meets something to whom he has given the name "God."

According to all we know, no community or culture has ever existed without religion. Religion has asserted itself among the most poorly developed races, and it lives its life-determining life among spiritually, intellectually, and morally advanced people of the highest education and in the highest cultures.

Religion proves to be a common element among people in all ages and to respond to a universal need. More correctly, it is a universal human experience. If one dares, then, to say something about the origin of religion, there is basically no better answer than that which religions themselves have given. It is attributed to a deity who has himself sought humanity out and entered into a union with humanity. It is from this experience and the relationship that comes into existence—summons and response—perceptions of a god enter humanity's consciousness. But it is given at the instant when the summons is perceived and gets a response. Humanity has, as we have seen above, hardly ever imagined sacred power except in union with some form of personal essence, regardless of what form this personal being is thought of. It is the summons of the external that stands behind the perceptions of God. In that sense, one can speak of an Ur-revelation—not as a one-time historical event, but as something that has happened since humans became humankind.

But about that which stands behind the summons, scholarship can say nothing. The furthest that scholarship can work back to is to assert that in human nature itself there must lie a universal fundament for religion. The Bible and religion say the same thing. Humans are created in God's image, and as Paul said, "For what can be known about God is plain to them, because God has shown it to them. Ever since the creation of the world his eternal power and divine nature, invisible though they are, have been understood and seen through the things he has made."[7] In religion's own language, it means that humans are created by God for God in order to live in community with him. Augustine expressed it in this way: "You made us, Lord, for yourself, and our hearts will be restless until we rest in you" (*Confessions* 1.1).

FOUNDATION AND REVELATION

How did this foundation become reality? If scholarship sets out to answer this question, it cannot, within the proper and necessary limits of its methods, go further than to say that religion has "developed from" or "arose from" that foundation in connection with certain spiritual and biological conditions. Scholarship can only deal with immanent, worldly factors. Beyond that, its ability to verify does not reach, and indeed it does not go beyond perceptible verification.

---

7. Rom 1:19–20a; van der Leeuw, *Phänomenologie*, 436–514 [ET: *Religion in Essence and Manifestation*, 459–539].

But can the reality simply result from possibility without something else getting involved? This does not seem logical, but from the side of thought and logic, in and of themselves, there should not be anything to prevent acceptance of the response that Christianity and all other religions give. Religion came into existence because God himself has met humanity and "made himself known." He has made himself known for humanity's religious foundation and for man's rational recognition. "God has indeed revealed himself," says Paul (Rom 1:19). Paul is speaking here not only of "revealed religion" in a special meaning, but about the universal religious realization that is possible for all people who will use their reason and that he acknowledged in all other religions.

Paul is here involved in the both psychologically and theologically obvious truth, that such a revelation happens through and with the help of those concepts, that view of reality and that thought procedure that shape the particular person, age, and culture. It is transmitted through humanity's own spiritual and intellectual equipment. God has made himself known wherever people have been able to perceive even the least part of God. All religions contain flashes of this.

Religion has come into being by God's creating humanity with a religious inclination and in one way or another making himself known to that religious inclination that is inherent to humanity. The origin of religion is revelation as the completion of creation. And this has happened at different times, in different places, and in different ways in the pre-history of the human race. There is not, as we have said, a people or culture without religion. In all religions there is a more or less clear glimpse of actual recognition of the divine.

The Problem of the Origin of Religion

PSYCHOLOGICAL-HISTORICAL MEDIATION: REVELATION HISTORY

But this approach has its psychological-historical side that scholarship can attempt to trace and describe.[8]

It is in the nature of the matter that whatever must have happened happened through the human soul and consciousness as a medium, and that it was, therefore, perceived, shaped, and expressed in the notions and according to the perception of reality of the particular period in question. And since the origin of religion lies before all history, it is clear that the oldest religion must have been perceived by humans and expressed in the categories and forms of the primitive, magical perception of life. This is the reason why so much of this perception of reality remains fixed in the old religions and their worship, and so often crops up in them.

This is also the reason why humanity's concrete notions about the God whom it has encountered differ so much with the times. God can be perceived as one and as many, in human or other form, with these or those characteristics, and so forth; and the forms of worship and the ideas of doctrine are truly legion.

But also because of that, there is a common thread in all of this variety. Revelation is not a one-time act, but a history. God's self-revelation is a history of revelation that empirically emerges as a history of spiritual life. All religions share in it. Theologians have spoken of this as the "universal revelation." But the line toward the goal is gathered around the religion of Israel and leads past it to Christianity—the special history of revelation.

THE ANSWER OF FAITH

The question of the origin of religion, like all questions about the most inner realities, comes up against a boundary where the scientific explanation must surrender. In doing so, it is in the same

---

8. Cf. van der Leeuw, *Phänomenologie*, 643ff. [ET: *Religion in Essence and Manifestation*, 671–95].

position as, for example, the question about what life is or what the meaning of life is. Thus humans are led from the viewpoint of causality to that of values and theology. The question about the essence of life is, in the final analysis, a question about its meaning and goal. And only from this point can light be shed on the question about its origin. But it is no longer the light of science, but rather the response of faith.

Nor can the question about the origin of religion finally be answered otherwise than from belief.

And here, we stand again in the presence of what religion's innermost essence is: belief that comes into existence in and with a summons from the Holy One, which is heard and received and encountered in trust and obedience—whether it happens in a very primitive perception or as frequently is imperfectly perceived. Religion itself knows that this is its "origin." And if we should wish some answer to how it came into existence, then we must find our answer in such a belief—a belief that accepts—hypothetically, as far as I am concerned—religion's own answer to what it is. It is that which it has always said that it is—and it should probably know that best—then it follows that it derives from that which it has always asserted itself to be derived from.

It is humanity's answer to God's eternal summons, it is created by his "word" and it finds, therefore, its fullness in him who is "the Word."

19 | Overview

Much of what has been said about worship in the preceding may seem strange to a modern Protestant, and it may seem especially odd to see the connection of ideas and the unquestionable historical relationship between Israel's worship and the other religions of the ancient Near East. There is concern here with things that are more or less common to all ancient worship and that are known from the universal history of religion and the phenomenology of religion. But it cannot be denied that certain universal elements of worship are also found in the Old Testament, and that even Israel's worship developed from the same general perception.

But it should not be difficult, either, to discover the essential elements in this picture of worship that are decisive for the Christian liturgy: fellowship, the religious experience of salvific acts—as the basis for it, the socially regulated rituals, places, times, cultic persons, and so forth; the spiritual content of power in the rites and words that are holy; the constantly renewing experience of the salvific foundation through which "the holy" is encountered, with God through liturgy and word; God as the one who actually takes the initiative even in the liturgy; his self-revelation and self-mediation through its sacramental elements; the yielding of the community and the individual to God through the stage of the sacrificial liturgy, the creating of life and the renewal of life in meeting God in the liturgy—the "dramatic" in this interchange in the liturgy and in the re-experiencing of salvation history both in the individual liturgy and in the liturgical calendar with its "highpoints in time"; the intention of all of this: to procure "life" and blessing for daily activity through communion with God in his visibly revealed sign (Christ), and so forth.

And these elements were also, in a more or less exotic and primitively working forms, essential in Israel's worship as well as that of Judaism. There God met the community, renewed his covenant with it and created its world anew. He relived the foundation of salvation, proclaimed and gave his blessing, made life secure for his people, pointed out their sin, made certain the fulfillment of their hope and gave them a future through a re-enactment of their past and the believing appropriation of the salvific activity that had been. And there God received the praise and thanksgiving of the community and their humble prayer.

This is that which ancient Israel experienced in its liturgy, and which the eye of faith experienced in all of those many, for us, strange and exotic individual rites that were handed down from prehistoric times, or taken over according to the pattern of worship in the universal Near Eastern culture in which Israel was fixed.

The believers in all religions have experienced some of this in their worship, each from their own historical, cultural, and religious conditions. It is quite necessary to see each religion as the peculiar structural unity that it is. All of its details receive their content and meaning from the unity of which they are members, not from what these parts mean in other systems or what meaning they might once have had in another culture.[1] But it is also necessary to see the common foundation and for the Christian witnesses that the "seed of the *logos*" always and everywhere has been sown, and that something has germinated and created a foundation for receiving the full message of the Word.[2]

---

1. Grønbech in *Illustreret Religionshistorie*, 15.
2. Cf. Reichelt, *Fromhetstyper og Helligdommer i Øst-Asia*, 1:29ff.

The Works of Sigmund Mowinckel in English

BOOKS

1937 *The Two Sources of the Predeuteronomic Primeval History (JE) in Genesis 1–11.* Avhandlinger utgitt av det Norske Videnskaps-Akademii Oslo. Oslo: Dybwad.

1946 *Prophecy and Tradition: The Prophetic Books in the Light of the Study of the Growth and History of the Tradition.* Oslo: Dybwad. [See 2002]

1956 *He That Cometh.* Translated by G. A. Anderson. Rev. ed. Nashville: Abingdon. Norwegian ed. 1951.

1957 *Real and Apparent Tricola in Hebrew Psalm Poetry.* ANVAO. Oslo: Dybwad.

1959 *The Old Testament as Word of God.* Translated by Reidar B. Bjornard. Nashville: Abingdon. Norwegian ed. 1938.

1962 *The Psalms in Israel's Worship.* 2 vols in 1. Translated by D. R. Ap-Thomas. Nashville: Abingdon. Norwegian ed. 1951.

1981 *Religion and Cult.* Translated by John F. X. Sheehan SJ. Milwaukee: Marquette University. Norwegian ed. 1950. German ed. 1953.

1992 *The Psalms in Israel's Worship.* 2 vols in 1. Translated by D. R. Ap-Thomas. Reprinted, with a new foreword by Robert K. Gnuse and Douglas A. Knight. Sheffield: JSOT Press.

2002 *The Spirit and the Word: Prophecy and Tradition in Ancient Israel.* Edited by K. C. Hanson. Fortress Classics in Biblical Studies. Min-neapolis: Fortress.

2004	*The Psalms in Israel's Worship.* 2 vols in 1. Translated by D. R. Ap-Thomas. Reprinted, with a new foreword by James L. Crenshaw. Biblical Resource Series. Grand Rapids: Eerdmans.
2005	*He That Cometh: The Messiah Concept in the Old Testament and Later Judaism.* Translated by G. A. Anderson. Rev. ed. With a new foreword by John J. Collins. Biblical Resource Series. Grand Rapids: Eerdmans.
2012	*Religion and Cult.* Translated by J. F. X. Sheehan SJ. Edited with a new foreword and bibliographies by K. C. Hanson. Eugene, OR: Cascade Books.

ARTICLES AND ESSAYS

1934	"The 'Spirit' and the 'Word' in the Pre-exilic Reforming Prophets." *Journal of Biblical Literature* 53:199–227.
1935	"Ecstatic Experience and Rational Elaboration in Old Testament Prophecy." *Acta Orientalia* 13:264–91.
1936	"Ecstatic Experience and Rational Elaboration in Old Testament Prophecy." *Acta Orientalia* 14:319.
1939	"The Babylonian Matter in the Predeuteronomic Primeval History (JE) in Gen. 1–11." *Journal of Biblical Literature* 58:87–91.
1950	"Traditionalism and Personality in the Psalms." *Hebrew Union College Annual* 23:205–31.
1953	"The Hebrew Equivalent of *Taxo* in *Ass. Mos.* ix." In *Congress Volume: Copenhagen, 1953*, 88–96. Vetus Testamentum Supplements 1. Leiden: Brill.
1955	"Psalms Criticism between 1900 and 1935." *Vetus Testamentum* 5:13–33.
1956	"Some Remarks on Hodayoth 39:5-20." *Journal of Biblical Literature* 75:265–76.
1957	"The Copper Scroll—An Apocryphon?" *Journal of Biblical Literature* 76:261–65.

The Works of Sigmund Mowinckel in English

1959   "General Oriental and Specific Israelite Elements in the Israelite Conception of the Sacral Kingdom." In *The Sacral Kingship*, 283–93. Studies in the History of Religions 4. Leiden: Brill.

1959   "Notes on the Psalms." *Studia Theologica* 13:134–65.

1961   "The Name of the God of Moses." *Hebrew Union College Annual* 32:121–33.

1961   "The Verb *siach* and the Nouns *siach* and *sicha*." *Studia Theologica* 15:110.

1962   "Drive and/or Ride in the O.T." *Vetus Testamentum* 12:278–99.

1962   "Legend." In *Interpreter's Dictionary of the Bible*, edited by G. A. Buttrick, 3:108–10. Nashville: Abingdon.

1962   "Literature." In *Interpreter's Dictionary of the Bible*, edited by G. A. Buttrick, 3:139–43. Nashville: Abingdon.

1962   "Tradition, Oral." In *Interpreter's Dictionary of the Bible*, edited by G. A. Buttrick, 4:683–85. Nashville: Abingdon.

1963   "Israelite Historiography." *Annual of the Swedish Theological Institute* 2:4–26.

1963   "Shachal." In *Hebrew and Semitic Studies: Presented to Godfrey Rolles Driver in Celebration of his Seventieth Birthday, August 20, 1962*, edited by D. W. Thomas and W. D. McHardy, 95–103. Oxford: Clarendon.

1967   "Mowinckel's Letter." *Luther Theological Seminary Review* 5/2:41–44.

MOWINCKEL'S COMPLETE BIBLIOGRAPHY

Kvale, Dagfinn, and Dagfinn Rian. "Sigmund Mowinckel: A Bibliography." *SJOT* 2 (1988) 95–168.

———. *Sigmund Mowinckel's Life and Works: A Bibliography*. With an introduction on Sigmund Mowinckel and Old Testament Study by Arvid S. Kapelrud. Leiden: Brill, 1984.

ASSESSMENTS OF MOWINCKEL'S WORK

Ap-Thomas, D. R. "An Appreciation of Sigmund Mowinckel's Contribution to Biblical Studies." *Journal Biblical Literature* 85 (1966) 315–25.

Barr, James. "Mowinckel, the Old Testament, and the Question of Natural Theology (The Second Mowinckel Lecture—Oslo, 27 November 1987)." *Studia Theologica* 42 (1988) 21–38.

Barstad, Hans M. "Some Aspects of Sigmund Mowinckel as Historian." *Scandinavian Journal of the Old Testament* 2 (1988) 83–91.

Collins, John J. "Foreword: Mowinckel's *He That Cometh* in Retrospect." In *He That Cometh: The Messiah Concept in the Old Testament and Later Judaism*, xv–xxviii. Translated by G. A. Anderson. Rev. ed. Biblical Resource Series. Grand Rapids: Eerdmans, 2005.

Clements, Ronald E. "Sigmund Mowinckel." In *Historical Handbook of Major Biblical Interpreters*, edited by D. K. McKim, 505–10. Downers Grove, Ill.: InterVarsity, 1998.

Dahl, Nils A. "Sigmund Mowinckel: Historian of Religion and Theologian." *SJOT* 2 (1988) 8–22.

Gnuse, Robert K., and Douglas A. Knight. "Foreword to the Reprint Edition." In *Sigmund Mowinckel, The Psalms in Israel's Worship*, xxi–xxviii. Biblical Seminar 14. Sheffield: JSOT Press, 1992.

Hauge, Martin Ravndal. "Sigmund Mowinckel and the Psalms—A Query into His Concern." *Scandinavian Journal of the Old Testament* 2 (1988) 56–71.

Hygen, Johan B. "Sigmund Mowinckel: The Man and the Teacher." *Scandinavian Journal of the Old Testament* 2 (1988) 1–7.

Jeppesen, Knud. "The Day of Yahweh in Mowinckel's Conception Reviewed." *Scandinavian Journal of the Old Testament* 2 (1988) 42–55.

Kapelrud, Arvid S. "Sigmund Mowinckel and Old Testament Study." *Annual of the Swedish Theological Institute* 5 (1967) 4–29.

———. "Sigmund Mowinckel's Study of the Prophets." *Scandinavian Journal of the Old Testament* 2 (1988) 72–82.

Knight, Douglas A. *Rediscovering the Traditions of Israel*. 3rd ed. Studies in Biblical Literature 16. Atlanta: Society of Biblical Literature, 2006. [169–71, 190–96]

Sæbø, Magne. "Crossing Borders: Five Norwegian Bible Scholars." In *Congress Volume: Oslo, 1998*, edited by André Lemaire and Magne Sæbø, 1–16 [7–11]. Vetus Testamentum Supplements 80. Leiden: Brill, 2000.

Recommended Readings

CHAPTER 1: RELIGION

Albertz, Rainer. *The History of Israelite Religion*. 2 vols. Translated by John Bowden. Old Testament Library. Louisville: Westminster John Knox, 1994.

Anderson, Gary A. "Introduction to Ancient Israelite Religion." In *New Interpreter's Bible*, edited by Leander E. Keck, 1:272–83. Nashville: Abingdon, 1994.

Betz, Hans Dieter, editor. *Religion Past and Present: Encyclopedia of Theology and Religion*. 12 vols. 4th ed. Leiden: Brill, 2007–.

Bodel, John, and Saul M. Olyan, editors. *Household and Family Religion in Antiquity*. Ancient World—Comparative Histories. Malden, MA: Blackwell, 2008.

Day, John. *Yahweh and the Gods and Goddesses of Canaan*. Journal for the Study of the Old Testament Supplement Series 265. Sheffield: Sheffield Academic, 2000.

Durkheim, Emil. *The Elementary Forms of the Religious Life*. Translated with an introduction by Karen E. Fields. New York: Free Press, 1995.

Eilberg-Schwartz, Howard. *The Savage in Judaism: An Anthropology of Israelite Religion and Ancient Judaism*. Bloomington: Indiana University Press, 1990

Eliade, Mircea, editor. *Encyclopedia of Religion*. 16 vols. New York: Macmillan, 1987.

———. *Patterns in Comparative Religion*. Translated by Rosemary Sheed. 1958. Reprinted, Lincoln: University of Nebraska Press, 1996.

Eliade, Mircea, and David Tracy, editors. *What Is Religion? An Inquiry for Christian Theology*. Concilium 136. New York: Seabury, 1980.

Hess, Richard S. *Israelite Religions: An Archaeological and Biblical Study*. Grand Rapids:

Milgrom, Jacob. *Studies in Cultic Theology and Terminology*. Studies in Judaism in Late Antiquity 36. Leiden: Brill, 1983.

Miller, Patrick D. *The Religion of Ancient Israel*. Library of Ancient Israel. Louisville: Westminter John Knox, 2000.

Recommended Readings

Miller, Patrick D., Paul D. Hanson, and S. Dean McBride, editors. *Ancient Israelite Religion: Essays in Honor of Frank Moore Cross.* Philadelphia: Fortress, 1987.
Söderblom, Nathan. *The Nature of Revelation.* Translated by Frederic E. Papp. New York: Oxford University Press, 1933.
Smith, Mark S. *The Origins of Israelite Monotheism.* Oxford: Oxford University Press, 2001.
Toorn, Karel van der, editor. *Dictionary of Deities and Demons in the Old Testament.* 2nd ed. Leiden: Brill, 1999.
———. *Family Religion in Babylonia, Ugarit, and Israel: Continuity and Changes in the Forms of Religious Life.* Studies in the History and Culture of the Ancient Near East 7. Leiden: Brill, 1996.
Widengren, Geo. *Religionsphänomenologie.* Translated by Rosemarie Elgnowski. De Gruyter Lehrbuch. Berlin: de Gruyter, 1969.
Zevit, Ziony. *The Religions of Ancient Israel: A Synthesis of Parallactic Approaches.* London: Continuum, 2001.

CHAPTER 2: THE MEANING OF CULT

Anderson, Gary A., and Saul M. Olyan, editors. *Priesthood and Cult in Ancient Israel.* Journal for the Study of the Old Testament Supplements 125. Sheffield: Sheffield Academic, 1991.
Balentine, Samuel E. *The Torah's Vision of Worship.* Overtures to Biblical Theology. Minneapolis: Fortress, 1999.
Brueggemann, Walter. *Worship in Ancient Israel: An Essential Guide.* Abingdon Essential Guides. Nashville: Abingdon, 2005.
Day, John, editor. *Temple and Worship in Biblical Israel.* Library of Hebrew Bible/Old Testament Studies 422. London: T. & T. Clark, 2005.
Haran, Menahem. *Temples and Temple Service in Ancient Israel.* Oxford: Clarendon, 1978.
Kapelrud, Arvid S. "Tradition and Worship: The Role of the Cult in Tradition Formation and Transmission." In *Tradition and Theology in the Old Testament,* edited by Douglas A. Knight, 101–24. Philadelphia: Fortress, 1977.
Kraus, Hans-Joachim. *Worship in Israel: A Cultic History of the Old Testament.* Translated by Geoffrey Buswell. Richmond: John Knox, 1966.
Olyan, Saul M. "Cult." In *Archaeology in the Near East,* edited by Eric M. Meyers, 2:79–86. Oxford: Oxford University Press, 1997.
Rowley, H. H. *Worship in Israel: Its Forms and Meaning.* Philadelphia: Fortress, 1967.

Recommended Readings

CHAPTER 3: MAGICAL VIEW OF REALITY & CHAPTER 4: MAGIC AND RELIGION

Albrechtson, Bertil. *History and the Gods: An Essay on the Idea of Historical Events as Divine Manifestations in the Ancient Near East and in Israel.* Coniectanea biblica: Old Testament Series 1. 1967. Reprinted, Winona Lake, IN: Eisenbrauns, 2011.

Belier, Wouter W. "Religion and Magic: Durkheim and the Année Sociologique Group." *Method and Theory in the Study of Religion* 7 (1995) 163–84.

Goode, William J. "Magic and Religion: A Continuum." *Ethnos* 14 (1949) 172–82.

Graf, Fritz. *Magic in the Ancient World*. Translated by Franklin Philip. Revealing Antiquity 10. Cambridge: Harvard University Press, 1997.

Hammond, Dorothy. "Magic: A Problem in Semantics." *American Anthropologist* 72 (1970) 1349–56.

Hill, Donald R. "Magic: Theories of Magic." In *Encyclopedia of Religion*, edited by Mircea Eliade, 9:89–92. New York: Macmillan, 1987.

Kuemmerlin-McLean, Joanne K. "Divination and Magic in the Religion of Ancient Israel: A Study in Perspectives and Methodology." PhD diss., Vanderbilt University, 1986.

———. "Magic (OT)." In *Anchor Bible Dictionary*, edited by David Noel Freedman, 4:468–71. New York: Doubleday, 1992.

Middleton, John. "Magic: Theories of Magic." In *Encyclopedia of Religion*, edited by Mircea Eliade, 9:81–89. New York: Macmillan, 1987.

Pasi, Marco. "Magic." In *The Brill Dictionary of Religion*, edited by Kocku von Stuckrad, 3:1134–40. Leiden: Brill, 2007.

Schäfer, Peter. "Magic and Religion in Ancient Judaism." In *Envisioning Magic: A Princeton Seminar and Symposium*, edited by Peter Schäfer and Hans G. Kippenberg, 19–44. Studies in the History of Religions 75. Leiden: Brill, 1997.

Scurlock, J. A. "Magic (ANE)." In *Anchor Bible Dictionary*, edited by David Noel Freedman, 4:464–68. New York: Doubleday, 1992.

Thompson, R. C. *Semitic Magic*. 1908. Reprinted, New York: Ktav, 1971.

Versnel, Hendrik S. "Some Reflections on the Relationship Magic–Religion." *Numen* 38 (1991) 177–97.

Wagner, Roy. "Totemism." In *Encyclopedia of Religion*, edited by Mircea Eliade, 14:573–76. New York: Macmillan, 1987.

Widengren, Geo. "Religion und Magie." In *Religionsphänomenologie*, 1–19.

CHAPTER 5: HOLINESS AND THE HOLY ONE

Budd, P. J. "Holiness and Cult." In *The World of Ancient Israel: Sociological, Anthropological, and Political Perspectives*, edited by R. E. Clements, 275–98. Cambridge: Cambridge University Press, 1989.

Recommended Readings

Eliade, Mircea. "Approximations: The Structure and Morphology of the Sacred." In *Patterns in Comparative Religion*, 1–37. Translated by Rosemary Sheed. 1958. Reprinted, Lincoln: University of Nebraska Press, 1996.

Gammie, John G. *Holiness in Israel*. Overtures to Biblical Theology. Minneapolis: Fortress, 1989.

Kugler, Robert A. "Holiness, Purity, the Body, and Society: The Evidence for Theological Conflict in Leviticus." *JSOT* 76 (1997) 3–27

Meyers, Carol. *Households and Holiness: The Religious Culture of Israelite Women*. Facets. Minneapolis: Fortress, 2

Milgrom, Jacob. "Holy, Holiness, OT." In *New Interpreter's Dictionary of the Bible*, edited by Katharine Doob Sakenfeld, 2:850–58. Nashville: Abingdon, 2007.

Monroe, Lauren A. S. *Josiah's Reform and the Dynamics of Defilement: Israelite Rites of Violence and the Making of a Biblical Text*. Oxford: Oxford University Press, 2011.

Wagner, Roy. "Taboo." In *Encyclopedia of Religion*, edited by Mircea Eliade, 14:233–36. New York: Macmillan, 1987.

Wells, Jo Bailey. *God's Holy People: A Theme in Biblical Theology*. Journal for the Study of the Old Testament Supplements 305. Sheffield: Sheffield Academic, 2000.

Widengren, Geo. "Tabu und Heiligkeit." In *Religionsphänomenologie*, 20–45.

Wright, David P. *The Disposal of Impurity: Elimination Rites in the Bible and in Hittite and Mesopotamian Literature*. SBL Dissertation Series 101. Atlanta: Scholars, 1987.

———. "Holiness (OT)." In *The Anchor Bible Dictionary*, edited by David Noel Freedman, 3:237–49. New York: Doubleday, 1992.

CHAPTER 6: FELLOWSHIP: GOD AND THE CONGREGATION

Balentine, Samuel E. *The Hidden God: The Hiding of the Face of God in the Old Testament*. Oxford: Oxford University Press, 1983.

Burnett, Joel S. *Where Is God? Divine Absence in the Hebrew Bible*. Minneapolis: Fortress, 2010.

Kaiser, Otto. "*Deus absconditus* and *Deus revelatus*: Three Difficult Narratives in the Pentateuch." In *Shall Not the Judge of All the Earth Do What Is Right? Studies on the Nature of God in Tribute to James L. Crenshaw*, edited by David Penchansky and Paul L. Redditt, 73–88. Winona Lake, IN: Eisenbrauns, 2000.

Kutsko, John F. *Between Heaven and Earth: Divine Presence and Absence in the Book of Ezekiel*. Biblical and Judaic Studies from the University of California, San Diego 7. Winona Lake, IN: Eisenbrauns, 2000.

Recommended Readings

Malina, Bruce J. "First-Century Personality: The Individual and the Group." In *The New Testament World: Insights from Cultural Anthropology*, 58–80. 3rd ed. Louisville: Westminster John Knox, 2001.

Terrien, Samuel. *The Elusive Presence: Toward a New Biblical Theology.* 1978. Reprinted, Eugene, OR: Wipf & Stock, 2000.

Triandis, Henry C. "Cross-Cultural Studies in Individualism and Collectivism." In *Nebraska Symposium on Motivation 1989*, edited by R. A. Diensbier and J. J. Berman, 41–133. Lincoln: University of Nebraska Press, 1990.

CHAPTER 7: RITES

Bell, Catherine. *Ritual: Perspectives and Dimensions.* New York: Oxford University Press, 1997.

Bergen, Wesley J. *Reading Ritual: Leviticus in Postmodern Culture.* Journal for the Study of the Old Testament Supplements 417. London: T. & T. Clark, 2005.

Brichto, H. C. "On Slaughter and Sacrifice, Blood and Atonement." *Hebrew Union College Annual* 47 (1978) 19–56.

Gorman, Frank H., Jr. *The Ideology of Ritual: Space, Time and Status in the Priestly Theology.* Sheffield: JSOT Press, 1990.

———. "Ritual Studies and Biblical Studies: Assessments of the Past, Prospects of the Future." *Semeia* 67 (1994) 13–36.

Grimes, Ronald L. *Beginnings in Ritual Studies.* Rev. ed. Studies in Comparative Religion. Columbia: University of South Carolina Press, 1995.

———, editor. *Readings in Ritual Studies.* Upper Saddle River, NJ: Prentice Hall, 1996.

Gruenwald, Ithamar. *Rituals and Ritual Theory in Ancient Israel.* Brill Reference Library of Judaism 10. Leiden: Brill, 2003.

Human, Dirk J., and Cas J. A. Vos, editors. *Psalms and Liturgy.* Journal for the Study of the Old Testament Supplements 410. London: T. & T. Clark, 2004.

Kemper, Theodore D. *Status, Power and Ritual Interaction: A Relational Reading of Durkheim, Goffman and Collins.* Burlington, VT: Ashgate, 2011.

Milgrom, Jacob. *Leviticus: A Book of Ritual and Ethics.* Continental Commentaries. Minneapolis: Fortress, 2004.

Olyan, Saul M. *Rite and Rank: Hierarchy in Biblical Representations of Cult.* Princeton: Princeton University Press, 2000.

Rappaport, Roy A. *Ritual and Religion in the Making of Humanity.* Cambridge Studies in Social and Cultural Anthropology 110. Cambridge: Cambridge University Press, 1999.

Rooke Deborah W. "The Day of Atonement as a Ritual of Validation for the High Priest." In *Temple and Worship in Biblical Israel*, edited by John Day, 342–64. Library of Hebrew Bible/Old Testament Studies 422. London: T. & T. Clark, 2005.

Smith, Jonathan Z. *To Take Place: Toward a Theory of Ritual.* Chicago Studies in the History of Judaism. Chicago: University of Chicago Press, 1987.

Recommended Readings

Soggin, J. Alberto. *Israel in the Biblical Period: Institutions, Festivals, Ceremonies, Rituals*. Edinburgh: T. & T. Clark, 2001.

Watts, James W. *Ritual and Rhetoric in Leviticus: From Sacrifice to Scripture*. Cambridge: Cambridge University Press, 2007.

Widengren, Geo. "Der Ritus." In *Religionsphänomenologie*, 209–57.

Zeusse, Evan M. "Ritual." In *Encyclopedia of Religion*, edited by Mircea Eliade, 12:405–22. New York: Macmullan, 1987

CHAPTER 8: THE GOALS OF WORSHIP

Goldingay, John. *Israel's Life*. Old Testament Theology vol. 3. Downers Grove, IL: InterVarsity Press, 2009.

Westermann, Claus. *Blessing in the Bible and the Life of the Church*. Translated by Keith R. Crim. Overtures to Biblical Theology. Philadelphia: Fortress, 1978.

9: THE CYCLE: THE RENEWAL OF LIFE

Day, John. "Resurrection Imagery from Baal to the Book of Daniel." In *Congress Volume: Cambridge, 1995*, edited by J. A. Emerton, 125–33. Vetus Testamentum Supplements 66. Leiden: Brill, 1997.

Eliade, Mircea. *The Myth of the Eternal Return*. Translated by Willard R. Trask. New York: Pantheon, 1954.

———. *Rites and Symbols of Initiation: The Mysteries of Birth and Rebirth*. Translated by Williard R. Task. 1958. Reprinted, with a new foreword by Michael Meade, Dallas: Spring, 1994.

Gane, Roy. *Ritual Dynamic Structure*. Gorgias Dissertations. Piscataway, NJ: Gorgias, 2004.

Hiebert, Theodore. "Myth in the OT." In *New Interpreter's Dictionary of the Bible*, edited by Katharine Doob Sakenfeld, 4:191–95. Nashville: Abingdon, 2009.

Kaiser, Otto, and Eduard Lohse. *Death and Life*. Biblical Encounter Series. Nashville: Abingdon, 1981.

Leeuw, Gerardus van der. "Primordial Time and Final Time." In *Man and Time*, edited by Joseph Campbell, 324–50. New York: Pantheon, 1959.

Wagenaar, Jan A. "The Priestly Festival Calendar and the Babylonian New Year Festivals: Origin and Transformation of the Ancient Israelite Festival Year." In *The Old Testament in Its World*, edited by Robert P. Gordon and Johannes C. de Moor, 218–52. Old Testament Studies 52. Leiden: Brill, 2005.

Recommended Readings

10: THE CREATING DRAMA

Gaster, T. H. "Drama: Ancient Near Eastern Ritual Drama." In *Encyclopedia of Religion*, edited by Mircea Eliade, 4:446–50. New York: Macmillan, 1987.

———. *Thespis: Ritual, Myth, and Drama in the Ancient Near East*. Rev ed. Garden City, NY: Doubleday, 1961.

MacAloon, John J., editor. *Rite, Drama, Festival, Spectacle: Rehearsals toward a Theory of Cultural Performance*. Philadelphia: Institute for the Study of Human Issues, 1984.

Redmond, James, editor. *Drama and Religion*. Themes in Drama 5. Cambridge: Cambridge University Press, 1983.

Schechner, Richard. "Drama: Performance and Ritual." In *Encyclopedia of Religion*, edited by Mircea Eliade, 4:436–46. New York: Macmillan, 1987.

Seow, C. L. *Myth, Drama, and the Politics of David's Dance*. Harvard Semitic Monographs 44. Atlanta: Scholars, 1989.

11: PROPHECY AND MYSTICISM

Blenkinsopp, Joseph. *A History of Prophecy in Israel*. Rev. ed. Louisville: Westminster John Knox, 1996.

Craffert, Pieter W. *The Life of a Galilean Shaman: Jesus of Nazareth in Anthropological-Historical Perspective*. Matrix: The Bible in Mediterranean Perspective 3. Eugene, OR: Cascade Books, 2008.

Dupré, Louis. "Mysticism." In *Encyclopedia of Religion*, edited by Mircea Eliade, 10:245–61. New York: Macmillan, 1987.

Eikemeier, Dieter. "Shamanism." In *The Brill Dictionary of Religion*, edited by Kocku von Stuckrad, 4:1717–25. Leiden: Brill, 2007.

Eliade, Mircea. "Shamanism: An Overview." In *Encyclopedia of Religion*, edited by Mircea Eliade, 13:201–8. New York: Macmillan, 1987.

———. *Shamanism: Archaic Techniques of Ecstasy*. Translated by Willard R. Trask. London: Arkana, 1989.

Harner, Michael J. *The Way of the Shaman: A Guide to Power and Healing*. San Francisco: Harper & Row, 1980.

Mowinckel, Sigmund. *The Spirit and the Word: Prophecy and Tradition in Ancient Israel*. Fortress Classics in Biblical Studies. Minneapolis: Fortress, 2002.

Nissinen, Martti. *Prophets and Prophecy in the Ancient Near East*. Edited by Peter Machinist. Writings from the Ancient World 12. Atlanta: Society of Biblical Literature, 2003.

Overholt, Thomas W. "Prophecy: The Problem of Cross-Cultural Comparison." *Semeia* 21 (1982) 55–78. Reprinted in *Community, Identity, and Ideology: Social Science Approaches to the Hebrew Bible*, edited by Charles E. Carter and Carol L. Meyers, 423–47. Sources for Biblical and Theological Study 6. Winona Lake, IN: Eisenbrauns, 1996.

Widengren, Geo. "Die Mystik." In *Religionsphänomenologie*, 517–45.

Recommended Readings

Wilke, Annette. "Mysticism." In *The Brill Dictionary of Religion*, edited by Kocku von Stuckrad, 3:1279–85. Leiden: Brill, 2007.
Wilson, Robert R. "Prophecy and Mysticism: A Reexamination." *Journal of Biblical Literature* 98 (1979) 321–37. Reprinted in *Community, Identity, and Ideology: Social Science Approaches to the Hebrew Bible*, edited by Charles E. Carter and Carol L. Meyers, 404–22. Sources for Biblical and Theological Study 6. Winona Lake, IN: Eisenbrauns, 1996.

12: THE CULTIC MYTH: BELIEF AND CONFESSION

Batto, Bernard F. *Slaying the Dragon: Mythmaking in the Biblical Tradition.* Louisville: Westminster John Knox, 1992.
Bolle, Kees W. "Myth: Overview." In *Encyclopedia of Religion*, edited by Mircea Eliade, 10:261–73. New York: Macmillan, 1987.
Eliade, Mircea. *Myth and Reality.* Translated by Willard R. Trask. World Perspectives 31. New York: Harper & Row, 1963
Fontenrose, Joseph. *The Ritual Theory of Myth.* Folklore Studies 18. Berkeley: University of California Press, 1966.
Gaster, T. H. *Thespis: Ritual, Myth, and Drama in the Ancient Near East.* Rev ed. Garden City, NY: Doubleday, 1961.
Lévi-Strauss, Claude. *Myth and Meaning.* 1978. Reprinted, Routledge Classics. London: Routledge, 2001.
McCurley, Foster R. *Ancient Myths and Biblical Faith: Scriptural Transformations.* Philadelphia: Fortress, 1983.
Oden, Robert A., Jr. "Myth and Mythology." In *Anchor Bible Dictionary*, edited by David Noel Freedman, 4:946–60. New York: Doubleday, 1992.
Ricoeur, Paul. "Myth: Myth and History." In *Encyclopedia of Religion*, edited by Mircea Eliade, 10:273–82. New York: Macmillan, 1987.
Rogerson, J. W. *Myth in Old Testament Interpretation.* Beihefte zur Zeitschrift für die alttestamentliche Wissenschaft 134. Berlin: de Gruyter, 1974.
Smith, Mark S. "Mythology and Myth-making in Ugaritic and Israelite Literatures." In *Ugarit and the Bible*, edited by George J. Brooke, 293–341. Ugaritisch-biblisch Literatur 11. Münster: Varit-Verlag, 1994.
Widengren, Geo. "Der Gottesglaube: Das Wesen des Hochgottes," and "Der Gottesglaube: Pantheismus, Polytheismus, Monotheismus." In *Religionsphänomenologie*, 46–92, 93–129.
Wyatt, Nicolas. *Myths of Power: A Study of Royal Myth and Ideology in Ugaritic and Biblical Tradition.* Ugaritisch-biblisch Literatur 13. Münster: Varit-Verlag, 1996.

Recommended Readings

13: CULTIC ACTIONS

Anderson, Gary A. *Sacrifices and Offerings in Ancient Israel: Studies in Their Social and Political Importance.* Harvard Semitic Monographs 41. Atlanta: Scholars, 1987.

Girard, René. *Sacrifice.* Translated by Matthew Pattillo and David Dawson. Breakthroughs in Mimetic Theory. East Lansing: Michigan State University Press, 2011.

———. *Things Hidden Since the Foundation of the World.* Translated by Stephen Bann and Michael Metteer. Stanford: Stanford University Press, 1987.

———. *Violence and the Sacred.* Translated by Patrick Gregory. Baltimore: Johns Hopkins University Press, 1977.

Heger, Paul. *The Three Biblical Altar Laws: Developments in the Sacrificial Cult in Practice and Theology: Political and Economic Background.* Beihefte zur Zeitschrift für die alttestamentliche Wissenschaft 279. Berlin: de Grutyer, 1999.

Modéus, Martin. *Sacrifice and Symbol: Biblical Shelamim in a Ritual Perspective.* Coniectanea Biblical: Old Testament Series 52. Stockholm: Almqvist & Wiksell, 2005.

Rogerson, John W. "Sacrifice in the Old Testament." In *Sacrifice*, edited by M. F. C. Bourdillon and M. Fortes, 45–59. London: Academic Press, 1980.

14: CULTIC WORDS

Widengren, Geo. "Heiliges Wort und Heilige Schrift." In *Religionsphänomenologie*, 546–73.

15: PRAYERS AND PSALMS

Aejmelaeus, A. *The Traditional Prayer in the Psalms.* Beihefte zur Zeitschrift für die alttestamentliche Wissenschaft 167. Berlin: de Gruyter, 1986.

Boda, Mark J., Daniel K. Falk, and Rodney A. Werline, editors. *Seeking the Favor of God.* 3 vols. Early Judaism and Its Literature 21–23. Atlanta: Society of Biblical Literature 2006. Vol. 1: *The Origins of Penitential Prayer in Second Temple Judaism.*

Vol. 2: *The Development of Penitential Prayer in Second Temple Judaism.*

Vol. 3: *The Impact of Penitential Prayer beyond Second Temple Judaism.*

Gerstenberger, Erhard S. *Psalms, Part 1, with an Introduction to Cultic Poetry.* Forms of the Old Testament Literature 14. Grand Rapids: Eerdmans, 1988.

———. *Psalms, Part 2, and Lamentations.* Forms of the Old Testament Literature 15. Grand Rapids: Eerdmans, 2001.

Kraus, Hans-Joachim. *The Theology of the Psalms.* Translated by Keith Crim. Continental Commentaries. Minneapolis: Augsburg, 1986.

Miller, Patrick D. *They Cried to the Lord: The Form and Theology of Biblical Prayer.* Minneapolis: Fortress, 1994.

Widengren, Geo. "Beichte, Busse und Gebet." In *Religionsphänomenologie*, 258–79.

16: WORSHIP AND MORALITY

Kenneson, Philip. "Gathering: Worship, Imagination, and Formation." In *The Blackwell Companion to Christian Ethics*, edited by Stanley Hauerwas and Samuel Wells, 55–69. 2nd ed. Blackwell Companions to Religion. Malden, MA: Blackwell, 2011.

Maccoby, Hyam. *Ritual and Morality: The Ritual Purity System and Its Place in Judaism*. New York: Cambridge University Press, 1999.

17: IMPURITY, SIN, AND PURIFICATION

Douglas, Mary. *Purity and Danger: An Analysis of Concept of Pollution and Taboo*. London: Routledge & Kegan Paul, 1966.

Hanson, K. C. "Blood and Purity in Leviticus and Revelation." *Listening: Journal of Religion and Culture* 28 (1993) 215–30.

———. "Sin, Purification, and Group Process." In *Problems in Biblical Theology: Essays in Honor of Rolf Knierim*, edited by Henry T. C. Sun et al., 167–91. 1997. Reprinted, Eugene, OR: Wipf & Stock, 2011.

———. "When the King Crosses the Line: Royal Deviance and Restitution in Levantine Ideologies." *Biblical Theology Bulletin* 26 (1996) 11–25.

Kiuchi, Nobuyoshi. *The Purification Offering in the Priestly Literature: Its Meaning and Function*. Journal for the Study of the Old Testament Supplements 56. Sheffield: JSOT Press, 1987.

Knierim, Rolf P. "On the Contours of Old Testament and Biblical Hamartiology." In *The Task of Old Testament Theology: Substance, Method, and Cases: Essays*, 416–67. Grand Rapids: Eerdmans, 1995.

Maccoby, Hyam. *Ritual and Morality: The Ritual Purity System and Its Place in Judaism*. New York: Cambridge University Press, 1999.

Milgrom, Jacob. *Cult and Conscience: The Asham and the Priestly Doctrine of Repentance*. Studies in Judaism in Late Antiquity 18. Leiden: Brill, 1976.

Toorn, Karel van der. *Sin and Sanction in Israel and Mesopotamia*. Studia Semitic Neerlandica 22. Assen: Van Gorcum, 1985.

Wright, David P. *The Disposal of Impurity: Elimination Rites in the Bible and in Hittite and Mesopotamian Literature*. SBL Dissertation Series 101. Atlanta: Scholars, 1987.

18: THE ORIGINS OF RELIGION

Bellah, Robert N. *Religion in Human Evolution: From the Paleolithic to the Axial Age*. Cambridge, MA: Belknap, 2011.

Recommended Readings

Girard, René. *Things Hidden Since the Foundation of the World*. Translated by Stephen Bann and Michael Metteer. Stanford: Stanford University Press, 1987.

———. *Violence and the Sacred*. Translated by Patrick Gregory. Baltimore: Johns Hopkins University Press, 1977.

Hamerton-Kelly, Robert G., editor. *Violent Origins*. Stanford: Stanford University Press, 1987.

Hinde, Robert A. *Why Gods Persist: A Scientific Approach to Religion*. 2nd ed. New York: Routledge, 2010.

Koester, Helmut. "ὑπόστασις." In *Theological Dictionary of the New Testament*, edited by Gerhard Kittel and Gerhard Friedrich, 8:572–89. Translated and edited by Geoffrey W. Bromiley. Grand Rapids: Eerdmans, 1972.

Lewis-Williams, J. David. *Conceiving God: The Cognitive Origin and Evolution of Religion*. London: Thames & Hudson, 2010.

Pearson, Birger A. "Hypostasis." In *Encyclopedia of Religion*, edited by Mircea Eliade, 6:542–46. New York: Macmillan, 1987.

Söderblom, Nathan. *The Living God: Basal Forms of Personal Religion*. Gifford Lectures 1931. London: Oxford University Press, 1933.

Bibliography

Albright, William Foxwell. *Archaeology and the Religion of Israel.* 1942. Reprinted, with a new introduction by Theodore J. Lewis. Louisville: Westminster John Knox, 2006.

———. *From Stone Age to Christianity.* 2nd ed. 1946. Reprinted, Eugene, OR: Wipf & Stock, 2003.

Alt, Albrecht. "Der Gott der Väter." In *Kleine Schriften zur Geschichte des Volkes Israel.* Munich: Beck, 1953, 1959 and 1964. [Translated as: "The God of the Fathers." In *Essays on Old Testament History and Religion,* 1–100. Translated by R. A. Wilson. Oxford: Blackwell, 1966.]

Andræ, Tor. *Mystikens Psykologi: Besatthet och Inspiration.* Stockholm: Sveriges Kristliga Studentrørelse, 1926.

Ankermann, Bernhard. "Die Religion der Naturvölker." In *Lehrbuch des Religionsgeschichte,* edited by P. D. Chantepie de la Saussaye et al., 1:131ff. 4th ed. Tübingen: Mohr/Siebeck, 1925.

Benedict, Ruth. *Patterns of Culture.* New York: Penguin, 1946. [2nd ed., 1959.]

Berggrav, Eivind. *Den Religiøse Følelse i Sundt Sjeleliv: En Analyse av Stemning og Sinnelag i Kristendomme.* Oslo: Aschehoug, 1927.

Bertholet, Alfred. *Götterspaltung und Gottervereinungen.* Sammlung gemeinverständlicher Vorträge und Schriften aus dem Gebiet der Theologie und Religionsgeschichte 164. Tübingen: Mohr/Siebeck, 1933.

———. *Die jüdische Religion von der Zeit Esras bis zum Zeitalter Christi.* Grundriss der theologischen Wissenschaften 2. Tübingen: Mohr/Siebeck, 1911.

———. "Kultus." In *RGG*², 3:1365–72. Tübingen: Mohr/Siebeck, 1929.

———. "Religionsgeschichtliche Ambivalenzerscheinungen." *Theologische Zeitschrift* 4 (1948) 1ff.

Birkeli, Emil. *Fedrekult: Fra Norsk Folkeliv i Hedensk og Kristen Tid.* Oslo: Dreyer, 1943.

———. *Religionshistorie: Formlære.* Oslo: n.p., 1948.

Birket-Smith, Kaj. *Kulturens Veje.* 2 vols. Copenhagen: Jespersen og Pio, 1941–52. [Translated as: *Paths of Culture: A General Ethnology.* Translated by Karin Fennow. Madison: University of Wisconsin Press, 1965.]

Bibliography

Briem, Efraim. *Babyloniska Myter och Sagor: Med Kulturhistorisk Inledning.* Stockholm: Natur och Kultur, 1927.

———. *På Trons Tröskel: Studier i Primitiv Religion.* Stockholm: Nature och Kultur, 1949.

Brun, Lyder. *Paulus' Kristelige Tanker: En Studiebok.* 2nd ed. Kristiania/Oslo: Aschehoug, 1929.

Buber, Martin. *Königtum Gottes.* Berlin: Schocken, 1932. [Translated as: *Kingship of God.* Translated by Richard W. Scheimann. New York: Harper, 1967.]

Chantepie de la Saussaye, P. D., Alfred Bertholet, and Edvard Lehmann, editors. *Lehrbuch des Religionsgeschichte.* 4th ed. Tübingen: Mohr/Siebeck, 1925.

Dorsey, George A. *The Arapaho Sun Dance: The Ceremony of the Offering Lodge.* Anthropological Series 4. Chicago: Field Columbian Museum, 1903.

Elbogen, Ismar. *Der jüdische Gottesdienst in seiner geschichtlichen Entwicklung.* 3rd ed. Grundriss der Gesamtwissenschaft des Judentums. Frankfurt: Kauffmann, 1931.

Engnell, Ivan. *Studies in Divine Kingship.* Uppsala: Almqvist & Wiksell, 1943. [2nd ed., 1967.]

Erman, Adolf. *Die Ägyptische Religion.* 2nd ed. Handbücher der Königlichen Museen zu Berlin 9. Berlin: Reimer, 1909.

———. *Die Literatur der Aegypter: Gedichte, Erzählungen und Lehrbücher aus dem 3. und 2. Jahrtausend v. Chr.* Leipzig: Hinrichs, 1923.

Frankfort, Henri et al., *The Intellectual Adventure of Ancient Man: An Essay of Speculative Thought in the Ancient Near East.* Chicago: University of Chicago Press, 1946.

———. *Kingship and the Gods.* Chicago: University of Chicago Press, 1946.

Frazer, James George. *The Golden Bough: A Study in Magic and Religion.* 12 vols. London: Macmillan, 1911–18.

Friedrich, Johannes. *Aus dem Hethitischen Schrifttum: Übersetzungen von Keilschrifttexten aus dem Archiv von Boghazköi.* 2 vols. Der Alte Orient. Leipzig: Hinrichs, 1925.

Fridrichsen, Anton. *Hagios-Qadoš: Ein Beitrag zu den Voruntersuchungen zur Christlichen Begriffsgeschichte.* Videnskaps-Akademiets Skrifter. Kristiania/Oslo: Dybwad, 1916.

Gennep, Arnold van. *Les Rites de Passage.* Paris: Nourry, 1909. [Translated as: *Rites of Passage.* Translated by Monika B. Vizedom and Gabrielle L. Caffe. London: Routledge & Paul, 1960.]

Gressmann, Hugo, editor. *Altorientalische Texte und Bilder zum Alten Testament.* 2nd ed. Berlin: de Gruyter, 1926. Reprinted, 1953.

Grønbech, Vilhelm Peter. *Primitiv Religion.* Stockholm: n.p., 1915.

———, editor. *Illustreret Religionshistorie.* 2nd ed. Copenhagen: Gad, 1948.

———. *Vor Folkaeet i Oldtiden.* 4 vols. in 3. Copenhagen: Pios, 1909–12.

Gunkel, Hermann. *Genesis.* 4th ed. Handkommentar zum Alten Testament. Göttingen: Vandenhoeck & Ruprecht, 1917. [Translated as: *Genesis.*

Bibliography

Translated by Mark E. Biddle. Foreword by Ernest W. Nicholson. Mercer Library of Biblical Studies. Macon, GA: Mercer University Press, 1997.]

Gunkel, Hermann, and Joachim Begrich. *Einleitung in die Psalmen: Die Gattungen der Religiösen Lyrik Israels.* Göttinger Handkommentar zum Alten Testament. Göttingen: Vandenhoeck & Ruprecht, 1933. [Translated as: *Introduction to Psalms: The Genres of the Religious Lyric of Israel.* Translated by James D. Nogalski. Mercer Library of Biblical Studies. Macon, GA: Mercer University Press, 1998.]

Heiler, Friedrich. *Das Gebet: Eine religionsgeschichtliche und Religionspsychologische Untersuchung.* 2nd ed. Munich: Reinhardt, 1920. [Translated as: *Prayer: A Study in the History and Psychology of Religion.* Translated and edited by Samuel McComb. New York: Oxford University Press, 1932.]

Heitmuller, Wilhelm. *Im Namen Jesu: Eine Sprach- u. Religionsgeschichtliche Untersuchung zum Neuen Testament, Speziell zur Altchristlichen Taufe.* Forschungen zur Religion und Literatur des Alten und Neuen Testaments 2. Göttingen: Vandenhoeck & Ruprecht, 1903.

Hertzberg, Hans Wilhelm. *Prophet und Gott: Eine Studie zur Religiosität des vorexilischen Prophetentums.* Beiträge zur Förderung christlicher Theologie 28. Gütersloh: Bertelsmann, 1923.

Hölscher, Gustav. *Die Propheten: Untersuchungen zur Religionsgeschichte Israels.* Leipzig: Hinrichs, 1914.

Hooke, S. H., editor. *Myth and Ritual: Essays on the Myth and Ritual of the Hebrews in Relation to the Culture Pattern of the Ancient East.* Oxford: Oxford University Press, 1933.

Hvidberg, Fleming Friis. *Graad og Latter i Det Gamle Testament.* Copenhagen: Lunos, 1938. [Translated as: *Weeping and Laughter in the Old Testament: A Study of Canaanite-Israelite Religion.* Translated by Niels Haislund. Edited by Frede Løkkegaard. Leiden: Brill, 1962.]

———. *Det Israelistiske Religions Historie.* Copenhagen: Munksgaard, 1943.

Jastrow, Morris. *Die Religion Babyloniens und Assyriens.* 2 vols. in 3. Giessen: Töpelmann, 1905-12. [English original: *The Religion of Babylonia and Assyria.* Handbooks on the History of Religions 2. Boston: Ginn, 1898.]

Johnson, Aubrey R. *The One and the Many in the Israelite Conception of God.* Cardiff: University of Wales Press, 1942.

Karsten, Rafael. *Naturfolkens Religion.* Stockholm: Nature och Kultur, 1926.

Kramer, Samuel Noah. *Sumerian Mythology: A Study of Spiritual and Literary Achievement in the Third Millennium B.C.* Memoirs of the American Philosophical Society 21. Philadelphia: American Philosophical Society, 1944.

Kristensen, W. Brede. *Livet fra døden: Studier over Aegyptisk og Gammel Graesk Religion.* Oslo: Gyldendal, 1925. [2nd ed., 1948. Translated as: *Life out of Death: Studies in the Religions of Egypt and of Ancient Greece.* Translated by H. J. Franken and G. R. H. Wright. Grand Rapids: Eerdmans, 1992.]

———. *Tro eller Overtro.* Skrifter/Etnologisk Samfunn. Oslo: Norli, 1946.

Bibliography

Lang, Andrew. *The Making of Religion*. 2 vols. 2nd ed. New York: Longmans, Green, 1900.
Lange, H. O. *Religiøse Texter fra det Gamle Aegypten*. Verdensreligionernes Hovedvaerker i Oversaettelse 3-4. Copenhagen: Marcus, 1921.
Leeuw, G. van der. *Phänomenologie der Religion*. Tübingen: Mohr/Siebeck, 1933. [Translated as *Religion in Essence and Manifestation: A Study in Phenomenology*. Translated by J. E. Turner. New Foreword by Ninian Smart. Princeton: Princeton University Press, 1986.]
Lehmann, Edvard. "Erscheinungs- und Ideenwelt der Religion." In *Lehrbuch des Religionsgeschichte*, edited by P. D. Chantepie de la Saussaye et al., 1:23-130. 4th ed. Tübingen: Mohr/Siebeck, 1925.
―――. *Religionens Värld: I Mänskligheten, i Människosjälen*. Stockholm: Nature och Kultur, 1926.
Lévy-Bruhl, Lucien. *Les fonctions mentales dans les societies inferieures*. Travaux de l'Année sociologique. Paris: Alcan, 1910. [Translated as: *How Natives Think*. Translated by Lilian A. Clare. 1926. Reprinted, Princeton: Princeton University Press, 1985.]
―――. *La mythologie primitive: Le monde mythique des Australiens et des Papous*. Travaux de l'Année sociologique. 2nd ed. Paris: Alcan, 1935. [Translated as: *Primitive Mythology: The Mythic World of the Australian and Papuan Natives*. Translated by Brian Elliott. St. Lucia: University of Queensland Press, 1983.]
Lindblom, Johannes. *Profetismem i Israel*. Stockholm: Svenska Kyrkans Diakonistyrelses, 1934. [Translated as: *Prophecy in Israel*. Philadelphia: Muhlenberg, 1962.]
Marett, R. R. *The Threshold of Religion*. London: Methuen, 1909. [2nd ed., 1914.]
Michelet, S., Sigmund Mowinckel, and Nils Messel. *Det Gamle Testament*. 4 vols. Oslo: Aschehoug, 1929-1955.
Moe, Moltke. *Mai og Minne*. Samlede Skrifter. Oslo: Aschehoug, 1926.
Mowinckel, Sigmund. "'Ånden' og 'Ordet' hos de Foreksilske Reformprofeter." *NTT* 36 (1935) 1-31. [Translated as "The 'Spirit' and the 'Word' in the Pre-exilic Reforming Prophets." *Journal of Biblical Literature* 53 (1934) 199-227. Reprinted in *The Spirit and the Word: Prophecy and Tradition in Ancient Israel*, edited by K. C. Hanson, 83-99. Fortress Classics in Biblical Studies. Minneapolis: Fortress, 2002.]
―――. *Le Decalogue*. Paris: Alcan, 1927.
―――. "Drama, religionsgeschichtlisches." In *RGG*², 1:2000-2003. Tübingen: Mohr/Siebeck, 1927.
―――. "Ekstatiske Innslag i Profetenes Opplavelser." *NTT* 49 (1948) 129-43; 193-221. [Originally published as "Ecstatic Experience and Rational Elaboration in Old Testament Prophecy." *Acta Orientalia* 13 (1935) 264-91; 14 (1936) 319.]
―――. *Die Erkenntnis Gottes bei den alttestamentlichen Propheten*. Supplements to NTT. Oslo: Grondahl, 1941.

Bibliography

———. *Det Gamle Testament soms Guds ord*. Oslo: Gyldendal, 1938. [Translated as: *The Old Testament as the Word of God*. Translated by Reidar B. Bjornard. New York: Abingdon, 1959.]

———. "Hypostasen." In *RGG²*, 2:2065-68. Tübingen: Mohr/Siebeck, 1928.

———. "Kadesj, Sinai og Jahve." *Norsk Geografisk Tidskrift* 9 (1942) 1-32.

———. *Kongesalmerne i det Gamle Testamente*. Kristiania/Oslo: Aschehoug/Nygaard, 1916.

———. *Offersang og Sangoffer: Salmediktningen i Bibelen*. Oslo: Aschenhoug, 1951. [Translated as *The Psalms in Israel's Worship*. 2 vols. in 1. Translated by D. R. Ap-Thomas. 1962. Reprinted with new Foreword by James L. Crenshaw. Grand Rapids: Eerdmans, 2004.]

———. "Om Nebiisme og Profeti." *NTT* 10 (1909) 185-227; 330-60.

———. "Oppkomsten av Profetlitteraturen." *NTT* 43 (1942) 65-111.

———. *Profeten Jesaia: En Bibelstudiebok*. Oslo: Aschehoug, 1925.

———. *Psalmenstudien*. 6 vols. Kristiania/Oslo: Dybwad, 1921-24.

Psalmenstudien I: Äwän und die individuellen Klagepsalmen. 1921.

Psalmenstudien II: Das thronbesteigungsfest Jahwäs und der Ursprung der Eschatologie. 1922.

Psalmenstudien III: Kultprophetie und prophetische Psalmen. 1923.

Psalmenstudien IV: Die technischen Termini in den Psalmen Überschriften. 1923.

Psalmenstudien V: Segen und Fluch in Israels Kult- und Psalmendichtung. 1924.

Psalmenstudien VI: Die Psalmdichter. 1924

———. "A quelle moment le culte de Jahvé à Jerusalem est-il officiellement devenu un culte sans images?" *Revue d'Histoire et de Philosophie Religieuses* 9 (1929) 197-216.

———. Review of Geo Widengren, *Religionens Värld: Religionsfenomenologiska Studier och Översikter*. *NTT* 47 (1946) 181-92.

———. *The Spirit and the Word: Prophecy and Tradition in Ancient Israel*. Edited by K. C. Hanson. Fortress Classics in Biblical Studies. Minneapolis: Fortress, 2002.

———. "Tronstigningssalmerne og Jahves Tronstigningsfest." *NTT* 18 (1917) 13-79.

———. "Zwei Beobachtungen zur Deutung der פעלי און." *Zeitschrift für die alttestamentliche Wissenschaft* 43 (1925) 260-62.

Musil, Alois. *Arabia Petraea*. 3 vols. Vienna: Hölder, 1908.

Nilsson, Martin P. *Primitive Kultur*. Copenhagen: Norstedt, 1926.

———. *Primitive Religion*. Religionsgeschichtliche Volksbücher für die Deutsche Christliche Gegenwart 3/13-14. Tübingen: Mohr/Siebeck, 1911.

Noth, Martin. *Das System der zwolf Stämme Israels*. Beiträge zur Wissenschaft vom Alten und Neuen Testament 52. Stuttgart: Kohlhamer, 1930. Reprinted, Darmstadt: Wissenschaftliche Buchgesellschaft, 1966.

———. *Überlieferungsgeschichtliche Studien* I. Schriften der Königsberger Gelehrten Gesellschaft. Geisteswissenschaftliche Klasse. Halle: Niemeyer, 1943. [Translated as: *The Deuteronomistic History*. Translated by Michael D. Rutter et al. Edited by David J. A. Clines. Journal for the Study of the

Bibliography

Old Testament Supplements 15. Sheffield: University of Sheffield, Dept. of Biblical Studies, 1981.]

Oesterley, W. O. E. *The Sacred Dance: A Study in Comparative Folklore.* Cambridge: Cambridge University Press, 1923.

Ording, Hans. *Estetikk og kristendom.* Oslo: Aschehoug, 1929.

Otto, Rudolf. *Das Heilige: Über das Irrationale in der Idee des Göttlichen und sein Verhältnis zum Rationalen.* Munich: Beck, 1936. [Translated as: *The Idea of the Holy: An Inquiry into the Non-Rational in the Idea of the Divine and Its Relation to the Rational.* Translated by John W. Harvey. 2nd ed. London: Oxford University Press, 1950.]

———. *West-östliche Mvstik: Vergleich und Untersuchung zur Wesensdeutung.* Gotha: Klotz, 1926. [Translated as: *Mysticism East and West: A Comparative Analysis of the Nature of Mysticism.* Translated by Bertha L. Bracey and Richenda C. Payne. New York: Macmillan, 1932.]

Otto, Walter, edtior. *Kulturgeschichte des Alten Orients.* Handbuch der Altertumswissenschaft 3/1. Munich: Beck, 1933.

Pallis, Svend Aage. *The Babylonian Akitu Festival.* Historisk-filologiske Meddelelser 12. Copenhagen: Høst, 1926.

Pedersen, Johannes. *Der Eid bei den Semiten: in seinem Verhältnis zu verwandten Erscheinungen sowie die Stellung des Eides im Islam.* Studien zur Geschichte und Kultur des islamischen Orients 3. Strassburg: Trübner, 1914.

———. *Israel: Its Life and Culture.* Translated by Aslaug Møller and A. I. Fausbøll. 1926–40. Reprinted, Atlanta: Scholars, 1991.

Pfister, Friedrich. "Kultus." In *Paulys Real-Encyclopädie der classischen Altertumswissenschaft*, edited by Wilhelm Kroll and Kurt Witte, 11:2106–94. Stuttgart: Metzler, 1922.

Quell, Gottfried. *Das kultische Problem der Psalmen.* Beiträge zur Wissenschaft vom Alten Testament 8. Stuttgart: Kohlhammer, 1926.

Quensel, Oscar. *Homiletik.* 3rd ed. Stockholm: Norstedt, 1910.

Rad, Gerhard von. *Das Formgeschichtliche Problem der Hexateuchs*, Beiträge zur Wissenschaft vom Alten und Neuen Testament 26. Stuttgart: Kohlhammer, 1938. [Translated as: "The Form-Critical Problem of the Hexateuch." In *From Genesis to Chronicles: Explorations in Old Testament Theology*, edited by K. C. Hanson, 1–58. Translated by E. W. T. Dicken. Fortress Classics in Biblical Studies. Minneapolis: Fortress, 2005.]

Rad, Gerhard von, Georg Bertram, and Rudolf Bultmann. "ζαω κτλ. " In *Theological Dictionary of the New Testament*, edited by Gerhard Kittel and Gerhard Friedrich, 2:832–75. Grand Rapids: Eerdmans, 1964.

Raknes, Ola. *Møtet med det Heilage: Ein Etterøknad um det Psykologiske Grunnlaget for Religion.* Kjempefakkel 48. Oslo: Gyldendal, 1927.

Reichelt, Karl Ludvig. *Fromhetstyper og Helligdommer i Øst-Asia.* Oslo: Dreyer, 1947. [Translated as *Meditation and Piety in the Far East: A Religious-Psychological Study.* Translated by Sverre Holth. Missionary Research Series 19. London: Lutterworth, 1953. Reprinted, Cambridge: James Clarke, 1953.]

Bibliography

Robinson, H. Wheeler. "The Hebrew Conception of Corporate Person." In *Werden und Wesen des Alten Testaments*, edited by Paul Volz et al., 49–62. Beihefte zur Zeitschrift für die alttestamentliche Wissenschaft 66. Berlin: Töpelmann, 1936.

Roeder, Günther. *Urkunden zur Religion des alten Ägypten*. Jena: Diederichs, 1915. 2nd ed., 1923. Reprinted, 1978.

Rost, Leonhard. *Die Vorstufen von Kirche und Synagoge im Alten Testament*. BWANT 24. 1938.

Ruud, Jørgen. *Guder og Fedre: Religionshistorisk Stoff fra Madagaskar*. Oslo: Aschehoug, 1947. [Translated as: *Society and Religion among the Forest Tribes in Madagascar*. 1948. Reprinted, Oslo: Solum, 2002.]

Schjelderup, Kristian. *Die Askese: Eine religionspsychologische Untersuchung*. Berlin: de Gruyter, 1928.

Schmidt, H. "Keruben-Thron und Lade." In *Eucharisterion: Studien zur Religion und Literatur des Alten und Neuen Testaments: Hermann Gunkel zum 60. Geburtstage, dem 23. Mai 1922*, edited by Hans Schmidt, 120–44. Forschungen zur Religion und Literatur des Alten und Neuen Testaments 36. Göttingen: Vandenhoeck & Ruprecht, 1923.

Schmidt, Wilhelm. *Der Ursprung der Gottesidee: Eine historisch-kritische und positive Studie*. Münster: Aschendorff, 1912. [Translated as: *The Origin and Growth of Religion: Facts and Theories*. Translated by H. J. Rose. London: Methuen, 1931.]

Schürer, Emil. *Geschichte des jüdischen Volkes im Zeitalter Jesu Christ*. Leipzig: Hinrichs, 1901–1909. [Translated as: *The History of the Jewish People in the Time of Jesus Christ*. Revised and edited by Geza Vermes and Fergus Millar. 3 vols. in 4 parts. Edinburgh: T. & T. Clark, 1973–87.]

Söderblom, Nathan. *Framande Religionsurkunder: I Urval och Oversattning*. 3 vols. in 4. Stockholm: Geber, 1908.

———. *Gudstrons Uppkomst: Studier Öfver Gudstrons Uppkomst*. Stockholm: Geber, 1914.

———. *Ur Religionens Historia*. Stockholm: Norstedt, 1915.

Stade, Bernhard. *Biblische Theologie des Alten Testaments*. 2 vols. Grundriss der theologischen Wissenschaften. Tübingen: Mohr/Siebeck, 1905.

Ström, Åke V. *Religion och Gemenskap: Studier I Religionssociologi*. Stockholm: Svenska Kyrkans Diakonistyrelses, 1946.

Thureau-Dangin, François. *Die sumerisch-akkadischen Konigsinschriften*. Vorderasiatische Bibliothek 1/1. Leipzig: Hinrichs, 1907.

Underhill, Evelyn. *Worship*. 1936. Reprinted, Eugene, OR: Wipf & Stock, 2002.

Ungnad, Arthur. *Die Religion der Babyloniens und Assyrer*. Jena: Diederich, 1921.

Wellhausen, Julius. *Reste arabischen Heidentums*. Berlin: de Gruyter, 1927.

Wetter, Gilles P. *Religion och Magi*. Bibelforskaren, 1917.

Weule, Karl. *Kultur der Kulturlosen: Ein Blick in die Anfange menschlicher Geistesbetatigung*. Stuttgart: Kosmos, 1910.

Bibliography

Widengren, Geo. *Religionens Ursprung*. Stockholm: Alders/Bonniers, 1925. [Reprinted, 1963.]

———. *Religionens Värld: Religionsfenomenologiska Studier och Översikter*. Stockholm: SKD, 1945. [2nd ed., 1953.]

Will, Robert. *Le Culte: Étude d'Histoire et de Philosophie Religieuses*. Strasbourg: Istra, 1925.

Witzel, Maurus. *Tammuz-Liturgien und Verwandtes*. Analecta Orientalia 10. Rome: Pontifical Biblical Institute Press, 1935.

Zimmern, Heinrich. *Babylonische Hymnen und Gebete*. Der Alte Orient 13/1. Leipzig: Hinrichs, 1911.

Index of Ancient Documents

ANCIENT NEAR EASTERN & GRECO-ROMAN DOCUMENTS

Gilgamesh Epic
XII:143–154   67

Odyssey
11   67

OLD TESTAMENT[1]

Genesis

1–2	61
1:14ff.	56
2:1ff.	56
2:7	11
2:9	61
2:23	13
3:22	61
8:20–21	57
8:22	73
8:31	105
9:4	12
14:7	68, 131
14:19–20	63
24:2	65
24:60	114
27	114
32:23–32	63
35:8	69
50:10–11	69

Exodus

3:2	41
3:5a	41
3:5b	41
4:24–26	47
12:25–27	92
15:25	68
16:7a	44
17:1–7	68
19–32	55
19:10–15	42
19:10	138
19:14	138
19:15	138
20:24	50, 55, 63
23:17	49
29:18	57
29:20	139
32:32	61
34:23	49

---

1. Numbers in brackets indicates the verse numbering of the Hebrew texts.

Index of Ancient Documents

Leviticus

1:9	57, 105
1:13	105
1:17	105
2:2	105
2:9	105
4:5	141
6:17—7:6	141
11:1–47	136
12	136
13–14	136
14:5	138
14:17	138
15:13	138
15:1–33	136
16	141
16:20–22	107
17:10–14	19
17:11	12
17:14	12
18:4–6	42
18:28	136
18:30	42
19:2–3	42
19:2	33
19:10	42
19:12	42
19:14	42
19:16	42
19:18	42
19:25	42
19:27	42
19:29	42, 136
19:31–32	42
19:31	68
19:34	42
19:36–37	42
20:6	68
20:7	42
20:22	136
20:24	42
20:26	42
20:27	68
21:6	42
21:15	42
26:31	105

Numbers

5:11–31	
5:19–23	125
6:22–27	115, 125
6:23	63
8:7	138
10:35	114
10:36b	115
14:10–12	136
15:17	138
19:9–10	138
19:11	136
20:1	69
20:22–29	69
22–24	114
28:2	105

Deuteronomy

4:4	118
5:33	47
6–30	118
6:5	40
10:8	63
14	136
16:14	136
16:16	49
18:11	68
20:24	99
21:5	63
21:7–9	125
23:1–3	49
23:13	136
26:1–10	125
26:12–15	125
26:14	137

Index of Ancient Documents

Deuteronomy (*cont.*)
26:56–59	96
27:14–26	125
30:11–14	125
31:9–13	133

Joshua
24	55
24:30	69

Judges
2:9	69
5	47
9:4	47, 55
9:6	55
9:13	105
9:46	47
10:25	69
12:7	69
12:10	69
12:12	69
12:15	69
13:5	138
13:14	138
14:16	138
14:19	138
16:1	69
16:17	19
19–21	48

1 Samuel
1:15	129
6:1—7:2	32
6:19–20	32
10:2	69
10:5–6	60
14:3c	43
14:37a	43
20:5–6	49
20:26–27	49
20:28–29	49
21	68
21:5–6	42
21:5	138
25:1	137
28:3–25	12
28:3	22, 68, 137
28:9	68
28:13	69

2 Samuel
5:1	13
5:8b	49
6:6–15	33, 44
6:6–7	32
6:11	44
9:13	64
19:12	13
21:3	136

1 Kings
2:34	137
13:2	136
17:1	73
18:30–45	99

2 Kings
2:20–21	138
3:15	60
5:10	138
9:22	23
13:14–19	116
21:6	68
23	55
23:14	136
23:16	136
23:20	136

1 Chronicle
25:1–30	123

Index of Ancient Documents

Ezra
3:64 — 47

Nehemiah
8:10 — 60

Psalms
2 — 127
6 — 145
6:5[6] — 69
6:7[8] — 137
6:8b–9[9b–10] — 145
8 — 91
15 — 49, 127, 133
16:3 — 137
16:11 — 61
19:8–9[9–10] — 137
21:4[5] — 61, 66
24 — 120, 127
24:3–6 — 49
24:5 — 55
27:13 — 61
29:1 — 64, 75, 122
29:10 — 75
29:11 — 75
30:9[10] — 69, 137
32 — 145
32:1–2 — 144
32:3–5 — 143
36:7–9[8–10] — 62
36:9[10] — 61
40 — 144
41:8[9] — 136
42:8[9] — 61
45:1[2] — 123
46:8–9[9–10] — 78, 82
48:8–9[9–10] — 78
48:8[9] — 82
49:3–4[4–5] — 123
49:7[8] — 66
50:13 — 109
51 — 144
51:17[18] — 109
52:5[7] — 61
55:23[24] — 66
56:8[9] — 61
65:12 — 56
68:11–14[12–15] — 112
69 — 144
69:13[14] — 56
69:28[29] — 61
74:8 — 56
76:2 — 83
81 — 119
82 — 126
84 — 55
85 — 118
87:7 — 55
88:10–12[11–13] — 69, 137
89:5[6] — 137
89:7[8] — 137
90:3–5 — 66
91:11 — 61
91:16 — 61
95 — 119
96:10 — 75
96:13 — 83
97:1 — 75
98:9 — 83
104:19 — 56
104:30 — 74
107 — 126
110 — 127
115 — 127
115:16–17 — 137
115:17 — 69
116:9 — 61
118:26 — 63
126:5 — 87
129:8 — 63
132 — 84, 127
132:7 — 44
133:3 — 55, 61

Index of Ancient Documents

Proverbs	
3:2	61
3:18	61
5:6	61
6:23	61
7:23	19
8:35–36	61
10:17	61
11:30	61
13:12	61
13:14	61
14:27	61
15:4	61
15:24	61

Isaiah	
1:4	33
1:10–27	109
1:11	109
6	108
6:5	30, 121
6:6–7	138
8:19	68
12:15	23
19:3	68
33:14–16	49
38:11	61
38:18–19	137
41:29	23
47:9	23
49:8	56
53:8	61
53:10	108
55:6	56
58:1–7	109
58:5	56
61:2	56
66:1–4	109
66:3	23

Jeremiah	
1:4–10	108
2:7	136
2:13	61
3:2	136
3:3	136
3:9	136
7	109
10:10	65
11:15	109
11:19	61
11:23	108
12:1–16	108
12:4	136
15:1–9	108
15:10–21	108
16:5–8	136
17:9–19	108
18:18–23	108
20:7–13	108
20:14–18	108
21:8	61
31:13	69

Ezekiel	
4–5	108
4:12–14	136
18:23	61
24:5–13	108
26:20	61
43:7–9	136
47:9	61

Hosea	
1	108
3	108
4:3	136
6:6	109
9:4	136–37
11:12	137

Index of Ancient Documents

Amos

2:12	138
4:41	109
5:4–5	109
5:4	61
5:5	23
5:6	61
5:14	61
5:18–27	109
5:21–25	109
7:17	136

Micah

6:6–8	49, 109

Habakkuk

1:12	73, 83
1:13	139

Haggai

2:12–14	33

Zechariah

5:5–11	142
14:8	61

APOCRYPHA

Sirach

17:27	137

Baruch

2:17–18	137

NEW TESTAMENT

Matthew

18:20	45

Luke

5:8	30, 121
18:13	129

John

4:10	61
6:33	61
6:38	61
6:45	61
7:38	61
17:3	70

Acts

2:28	61
17	30

Romans

1:19–20a	153
1:19	154
8:29	46
10:9	96

1 Corinthians

8:5	38
11:26	97
15:3	97

1 Timothy

1:17	65

James

2:19	1

Index of Ancient Documents

EARLY CHRISTIAN DOCUMENTS

Ignatius of Antioch
To the Ephesians
2:20   71

Index of Subjects

Aaronic blessing, 15
Aborigines, 5-6, 10, 16, 21, 48,
    50, 67, 85, 87-88, 92-93,
    112, 123, 131, 149,
    151-52
Abraham, 39, 53, 95
Achilles, 67
acknowledgment of sin,
    143-44, 146
actualization, 13, 71, 77, 80,
    83, 93
Adonis, 35
African tribes, 16, 37, 149-50
All Souls Day Festival, 67
Amesha Spentas, 36
amphictyony, 46-47,
Anat, 35, 39, 80
ancestor veneration, 36, 68-69,
    137, 148, 150, 152
angels, 40, 91
animatism, 11, 18
animism, 4, 11, 18, 148
Anu, 151
Apostles' Creed, 97
Arabs, 43, 53, 69
Arctic tribes, 32
ark of the covenant, 32, 43-44,
    52, 74, 81, 84, 114
Assyria, 93, 123, 143
Augustine, 153

Ba'al, 35, 39, 47, 73, 78, 80, 118
Babylonia, 20, 35, 37, 54-55, 67,
    74, 79, 93-94, 97, 108,
    112, 116, 118, 120, 123,
    139, 141-44, 150-51
Balaam, 114
baptism, 48, 97, 113
blessing, 9, 32, 37, 39, 44,
    50-51, 53, 55, 57, 63-68,
    72-75, 83, 87-88, 93, 96,
    100-102, 104-5, 107,
    112-22, 126-27, 132,
    142, 158
blood, 12-13, 19, 34, 48, 102,
    107-9, 138-39, 141
Botocudo tribe, 10
bread of presence, 57
bread of life, 61
Buddha, 6
Buddhism, 5-6, 96

Canaan/Canaanites, 9, 39, 44,
    54, 56, 65, 68, 73, 76, 78,
    82-83, 87-88, 93, 104,
    108, 112, 118, 137, 151
causality, 10-11, 14-15, 17, 156
chaos, 73, 75, 79-80, 84-86, 93,
    112, 125, 136
chief, 13, 22, 36-37, 53, 64
Christianity, x, 1-3, 9, 37,
    48-49, 59, 66, 70-71,

Index of Subjects

Christianity (*cont.*)
    82, 90, 94, 96–97, 101–2,
    113, 119–20, 130, 144,
    154–55, 157–58
Christmas, 82, 94
circumcision, 47–48
confession, 1, 3, 92–97, 125,
    129, 144, 146
cosmos, 73, 80, 131
covenant, 12–13, 39, 46–48, 50,
    55, 73, 75–76, 83–85, 89,
    94–95, 99, 102, 104, 119,
    124–25, 132–33, 158
creation, 32, 56, 74–75, 77–81,
    83, 85–86, 93–94, 125,
    153–54
creation epic/myth, 79, 94, 97,
    116, 118
cult of the dead, 36, 66, 68
cultic/temple prophets, 88–89,
    112, 116–19, 127, 145

Dagan, 35, 39
dance, 5, 15, 60, 77–79, 100,
    102–3, 113,
David, 32, 44, 47, 57, 84, 137
Day of Atonement, 141–42
Decalogue, 133
demons, 1, 18–19, 22–24, 40,
    52, 136, 142
Deutero-Isaiah, 96, 108
Dionysius, 104
drama, 15, 77–86, 93–94, 98,
    100, 116, 118–20, 127,
    157
dromena, 98
dynamism, 4

Easter, 82, 84
ecstasy, 43, 54, 59–61, 78,
    87–91, 99, 113

El, 118, 151
'el, 34
Elijah, 99
Elisha, 115
'elohim, 37, 69
ellu, 139
Enthronement Festival, 83, 86,
enthronement psalms, 75, 81
entrance regulations, 133
eschatology, 86
eternal life, 66–71
ethics, 1–2, 130, 132–33
Eucharist (*see* Lord's Supper)
exodus from Egypt, 83–85, 92,
    94

faith, 1–2, 5, 82, 85, 94–96
fasting, 142
fear of God, 30
Feast of Tabernacles, 56, 74, 103
fellowship, 1, 7–8, 45–51, 59,
    64, 69–71, 101–2, 104,
    121, 131, 157
fertility, 9, 32, 35–37, 64–65,
    68, 72, 75, 80, 83, 102,
    150–51
fertility cults, 78–80, 85, 102,
    106
fertility gods/goddesses, 35, 39,
    74, 79, 108, 137, 151
fetish, 31, 43–44, 148
fire, 20–21, 111, 138
forgiveness, 100, 108, 143–46
full moon, 20, 56

Gathas, 123
Gilgamesh Epic, 67
grave, 36–37, 66–70, 79
Gudea of Lagash, 22

Index of Subjects

Hannah, 129
henotheism, 38–39
holiness, 29–44, 49–51, 53–54,
   94, 100, 112, 118, 131,
   139, 148,
honor and shame, 14, 19, 36,
   39, 53, 64, 105–6, 108,
   114, 121–22, 143
Horus, 37, 79, 94
hypostases, 149

ilu, 34
Ignatius of Antioch, 71
inspiration, 123, 128
Isaiah, 30, 42, 82, 95–96, 115
Ishtar, 35, 74, 80, 116
Islam, 37, 70, 90, 96–97, 129

Jacob, 53, 63
Jerusalem, 32, 55, 57, 84, 106,
   117, 143–44
Job, 94, 96
Judaism, 3, 9, 37, 47, 54, 66,
   70, 74, 85–86, 96–97,
   106–7, 118, 125, 128–29,
   131–32, 134, 142, 158

Kadesh, 47, 54–55, 68, 131, 137,
kahin, 53
Kettu, 36
king (*see also* sacral kingship),
   13, 37, 53–54, 57, 64,
   66–67, 75–76, 79, 81,
   83–84, 102, 115, 117,
   125–27, 132, 141–42, 150
kohen, 53
korrobori, 5

Laestadian movement, 59
lament/lamentation, 79–80,
   120, 123, 126, 143, 145

leges sacrae, 49, 133
Levites, 54, 63
life, 72–76
Lord's Supper, 43, 49, 71

Ma'at, 36
magic, 4, 8–28, 33, 36, 44,
   62, 65, 77, 98–99, 107,
   112, 121–23, 128, 142,
   147–48, 150–52, 155
magician, 99
mana, 17–19, 21, 23, 31, 34–35,
   65, 138, 148
Manitu, 34, 88, 150
Marduk, 79, 94, 97
Marduk Festival, 79
maskil, 131
medicine man, 20–22, 36, 53,
   123
Misharu, 36
monolatry, 40
monotheism, 38–40, 149
moon, 20, 40, 56, 151
morning offering, 57
Moses, 9, 36, 41, 50, 53, 112,
   118, 137,
Mot, 39, 68, 73, 78, 80,
mother goddess, 35, 79
mysticism, 40, 90–91
myth, 1, 10, 14, 16, 74, 79–80,
   85, 92–98, 116–19, 120,
   123, 130

navel of the world, 74
Nazirites, 108, 138
new moon, 56
New Year Festival, 56, 79, 81,
   85, 87, 117–18, 132, 142,
Nicene Creed, 97
nkisi bags, 31

Index of Subjects

oath, 65
Odyssey, 67
offering, 57, 64, 101, 102–9, 115, 123, 125–26, 138, 141, 143–45
oil, 102, 118, 138–39
oracle, 12, 40, 46, 50, 53–54, 68, 111, 116–17, 127, 131
Orthodox Church, 97
Osiris, 37, 67–68, 79

pantheism, 38, 40
Passover, 92, 104
peace offerings, 104
penitential psalms, 143
Pentateuch, 118, 124, 141
Pentecostal assemblies, 59
Persians, 32, 67, 138
pharmakon aphthanasias, 71
Phoenicia, 80
piety, 24–25, 29, 109, 121
Pirqe Aboth, 74
Plato, 13
polydaimonism, 38
polytheism, 38, 40
pondus, 106
power, 1, 5–6, 9–13, 16–24, 26–40, 43–45, 48, 51–56, 59–60, 62–70, 72–75, 77–80, 83–89, 91, 93, 98–107, 112–16, 121, 126, 128, 130
prayer, 2–3, 24, 55, 61, 70, 99, 101, 103, 106, 116–17, 120–29, 141–45, 149, 151, 158
priest, 9, 13, 20, 22–23, 47, 53–54, 57–59, 63–64, 104, 106–7, 114–15, 117, 120, 124, 127, 139, 141–43, 145–46

profane, 29–31, 36, 50, 139,
prophet, 9, 12, 53–54, 59–60, 85, 88–91, 97, 108–9, 112–13, 115–19, 127, 129, 133–34, 140, 145
psalm, 3, 9, 57, 75, 78, 81, 83, 94, 105–6, 109, 112–13, 120–29, 131–32, 143–45
purification offering, 107, 126, 138, 141

qadosh, 30, 33, 139

rainmaking, 99
Reformation, 96
repentance, 106–7, 125
resurrection, 48, 70–71, 79–80, 83, 87, 118, 120
revelation, 26, 63, 76, 89, 95, 118–20, 124, 128, 131–32, 140, 153–56
rite, ritual, 2, 5–7, 10, 13, 16, 24–25, 27, 33, 35, 44, 46–50, 52–54, 59, 62, 64, 67–68, 77–79, 80–83, 88, 90, 92–93, 95, 98–100, 102–3, 108, 111–12, 114–17, 120, 122–24, 126, 129, 132–34, 139–42, 144–45, 149, 151–52, 157–58

Sabbath, 20, 56
sacral kingship, 37, 40, 150
sacramentals, 7, 60, 101–3, 120, 127–28
sacraments, 7, 101–3, 142
sacred laws, 133
sacred marriage, 79–80

Index of Subjects

sacrifice, 3, 7, 24, 31, 50, 52–53, 64, 74, 99–104, 106–7, 109–10, 114, 124, 144
Sadducees, 70
salat, 129
salt, 102, 138
Samuel, 129
sancire, 30
sanctus, 30
Saul, 12
scapegoat, 107, 142
sect, 2, 46, 70
Sedeq, 36
seer, 53–54
seer-priest, 13, 54
Seth, 37, 79, 94
sexual tabus, 131
shaman, 20, 22, 53, 59, 123
Shang Ti / T'ien, 151
Shechem, 55
Sheol, 66, 70, 137
Sinai, 47, 54–55, 68, 76, 119, 133
sin offering, 107, 138, 141, 145
Sioux Indians, 88
sorcery, 11, 22–24, 52, 136
speaking in tongues, 59
Sumerians, 22, 37, 74, 123
symbol, 7, 14–15, 21, 43–44, 48, 74, 77–78, 81–82, 88, 98–103, 110–13, 115, 142, 145
synagogue, 47, 97, 119–20

tabu, 19–20, 32–33, 37, 43, 56, 108, 130–32, 138–40
tahor, 135
talisman, 31
Tammuz, 35, 79, 120
Taoism, 25

temple, 9, 54–55, 57–58, 75, 80–81, 83, 88, 106, 120, 141–42
Ten Commandments (*see* Decalogue)
thankoffering, 126, 145
thanksgiving psalm, 126, 145
Tiamat, 79, 94
torah, 54
totem/totemism, 5–6, 16, 36, 92–93, 113, 148, 150, 152
truth, 36

Ugarit, 80
Urim and Thummim, 43, 54,

Vedas, 74, 123, 131
Vedic religion, 128
veneration of ancestors (*see* ancestor veneration)

Wakanda, 34–35, 88, 150
water, 21, 60, 61, 68, 99, 102–3, 113, 128, 138
Weltanschauung (worldview), 11, 17, 24
wine, 105, 113, 138
wisdom, 21–22, 68, 131, 144

Yahweh, 12–13, 32–37, 39–44, 47–48, 50, 54, 56–57, 63–65, 69–70, 73–76, 78, 81–85, 87–92, 95–96, 99, 102–9, 112–20, 125–27, 129, 132–33, 137, 139–45, 151

Zion, 55, 83

Index of Authors

Aejmelaeus, A., 171
Albertz, Rainer, 163
Albrechtson, Bertil, 165
Albright, William Foxwell, 10, 25, 137, 175
Alt, Albrecht, 39, 175
Anderson, Gary A., 163–64, 171
Andræ, Tor, 90, 175
Ankermann, Bernhard, 10, 20, 52, 175

Balentine, Samuel E., 164, 166
Batto, Bernard F., 170
Begrich, Joachim, 124, 127, 145, 177
Belier, Wouter W., 165
Bell, Catherine, 167
Bellah, Robert N., 172
Benedict, Ruth, 18, 175
Bergen, Wesley J., 167
Berggrav, Eivind, 31, 175
Berman, J. J., 167
Bertholet, Alfred, 7, 26, 31, 141, 149, 175
Bertram, Georg, 180
Betz, Hans Dieter, 163
Birkeli, Emil, 14, 16, 21, 25, 36, 69, 148, 175
Birket-Smith, Kaj, x, 16, 22, 46, 48, 72, 175

Blenkinsopp, Joseph, 169
Boda, Mark J., 171
Bodel, John, 163
Bolle, Kees W., 170
Brichto, H. C., 167
Briem, Efraim, x, 8, 16, 20–21, 31, 33, 35–36, 74, 99, 151, 176
Brooke, George J., 170
Brueggemann, Walter, 164
Brun, Lyder, 48, 176
Brun, N. J., 128
Buber, Martin, 92, 176
Burnett, Joel S., 166
Bultmann, Rudolf, 180

Chantepie de la Saussaye, P. D., 14, 52, 67, 175–76, 178
Clines, David J. A., 179
Crenshaw, James L., 159, 179

Day, John, 163–64, 167–68
Diensbier, R. A., 167
Dorsey, George A., 78, 176
Douglas, Mary, 172
Dupré, Louis, 169
Durkheim, Emil, 163

Eilberg-Schwartz, Howard, 163
Elbogen, Ismar, 47, 176

Index of Authors

Eliade, Mircea, 163, 165–66, 168–70, 173
Emerton, J. A., 168
Engnell, Ivan, 37, 176
Erman, Adolf, 79, 123, 176

Falk, Daniel K., 171
Fontenrose, Joseph, 170
Frankfort, Henri, 10, 37, 68, 79, 142, 148, 176
Frazer, James George, 11, 62, 176
Freedman, David Noel, 165–66, 170
Friedrich, Gerhard, 173
Friedrich, Johannes, 123, 176, 180
Fridrichsen, Annton, 176

Gammie, John G., 166
Gane, Roy, 168
Gaster, T. H., 169–70
Gennep, Arnold van, 72, 176
Gerstenberger, Erhard S., 171
Girard, René, 171, 173
Goldingay, John, 168
Goode, William J., 165
Gordon, R. P., 168
Gorman, Frank H., Jr., 167
Graf, Fritz, 165
Gressmann, Hugo, 74, 176
Grimes, Ronald L., 167
Grønbech, Vilhelm Peter, x, 1036, 73, 79, 105, 158, 176
Gruenwald, Ithamar, 167
Gunkel, Hermann, ix, 37, 92, 124, 127, 143, 145, 176–77

Hamerton-Kelly, Robert G., 173
Hammond, Dorothy, 165
Hanson, K. C., 159, 172, 178–80
Hanson, Paul D., 164
Haran, Menahem, 164
Harner, Michael J., 169
Hauerwas, Stanley, 172
Heger, Paul, 171
Heiler, Friedrich, 61, 121–22, 128, 177
Heitmuller, Wilhelm, 112, 177
Hertzberg, Hans Wilhelm, 129, 177
Hess, Richard S., 163
Hiebert, Theodore, 168
Hill, Donald R., 165
Hinde, Robert A., 173
Hölscher, Gustav, 88, 177
Hooke, S. H., 77, 79, 177
Human, Dirk J., 167
Hvidberg, Fleming Friis, 43–44, 65, 68, 73, 80, 87, 118, 177

Jastrow, Morris, 123, 177
Johnson, Aubrey R., 38, 177

Kaiser, Otto, 166, 168
Kapelrud, Arvid S., 161, 164
Karsten, Rafael, 10, 177
Kemper, Theodore D., 167
Kenneson, Philip, 172
Kittel, Gerhard, 173, 180
Kiuchi, Nobuyoshi, 172
Knierim, Rolf P., 172
Knight, Douglas A., 159, 161, 164
Koester, Helmut, 173
Kramer, Samuel Noah, 74, 177
Kraus, Hans-Joachim, 164, 171

Index of Authors

Kristensen, W. Brede, 25, 68, 177
Kuemmerlin-McLean, Joanne K., 165
Kugler, Robert A., 166
Kutsko, John F., 166

Lang, Andrew, 148, 150, 178
Lange, H. O., 123, 178
Leeuw, Gerardus van der, x, 7, 14, 16–17, 20, 24, 30–31, 36, 39, 45–46, 48, 50, 53–55, 59, 61–62, 66, 72, 77, 92, 98, 108, 121, 130, 135, 138, 140, 146, 150, 153, 155, 168, 178
Lehmann, Edvard, 7, 24, 30, 176, 178
Lévi-Strauss, Claude, 170
Lévy-Bruhl, Lucien, 10, 16, 178
Lewis-Williams, J. David, 173
Lindblom, Johannes, 60, 178
Lohse, Eduard, 168

MacAloon, John J., 169
Maccoby, Hyam, 172
Machinist, Peter, 169
Malina, Bruce J., 167
Marett, R. R., 18, 178
McBride, S. Dean, 164
McCurley, Foster R., 170
Messel, Nils, xiii, 178
Meyers, Carol, 166, 169–70
Meyers, Eric M., 164
Michelet, S., xiii, 178
Middleton, John, 165
Milgrom, Jacob, 163, 166–67, 172,
Millar, Fergus, 181
Miller, Patrick D., 163–64, 171
Modéus, Martin, 171

Moe, Moltke, 10, 178
Monroe, Lauren A. S., 166
Moor, Johannes C. de, 168
Mowinckel, Sigmund, ix–ix, xiii, 7, 14, 22–24, 32, 35, 37, 43–44, 49, 52, 57, 60, 63–64, 68, 75–76, 79, 81, 86, 88–89, 91–92, 95, 105, 115, 128, 132–33, 143, 145, 148–49, 159–61, 169, 178–79
Musil, Alois, 69, 179

Nilsson, Martin P., 10, 24, 49, 111, 179
Nissinen, Martti, 169
Noth, Martin, 47, 118, 179

Oden, Robert A., Jr., 170
Oesterley, W. O. E., 78, 180
Olyan, Saul M., 163–64, 167
Ording, Hans, 122, 180
Otto, Rudolf, 29–30, 41, 90, 180
Otto, Walter, 123, 180

Pallis, Svend Aage, 142, 180
Pearson, Birger A., 173
Pedersen, Johannes, x, 23, 30, 44–45, 55, 61, 63, 65, 69, 72, 80, 101, 112, 135–36, 140–41, 180
Penchansky, David, 166
Pfister, Friedrich, 7, 180

Quell, Gottfried, 7, 27, 50, 101, 180
Quensel, Oscar, 101, 180

Rad, Gerhard von, 95, 180
Raknes, Ola, 60, 180
Rappaport, Roy A., 167

Index of Authors

Redditt, Paul L., 166
Redmond, James, 169
Reichelt, Karl Ludvig, 158, 180
Ricoeur, Paul, 170
Robinson, H. Wheeler, 45, 181
Roeder, Günther, 123, 181
Rogerson, J. W., 170-71
Rooke Deborah W., 167
Rost, Leonhard, 46-48, 181
Rowley, H. H., 164
Ruud, Jørgen, 69, 181

Sakenfeld, Katharine Doob, 166, 168
Schäfer, Peter, 165
Schechner, Richard, 169
Schjelderup, Kristian, 138, 181
Schmidt, H., 44, 181
Schmidt, Wilhelm, 148-49, 181
Schürer, Emil, 47-48, 181
Scurlock, J. A., 165
Seow, C. L., 169
Smith, Jonathan Z., 167
Smith, Mark S., 164, 170
Söderblom, Nathan, 18, 29-30, 48-50, 92, 123, 132, 150, 164, 173, 181
Soggin, J. Alberto, 168
Stade, Bernhard, 69, 136-38, 140-41, 181
Ström, Åke V., 45, 181
Sun, Henry T. C., 172

Terrien, Samuel, 167
Thompson, R. C., 165
Thureau-Dangin, François, 22, 181

Toorn, Karel van der, 164, 172
Tracy, David, 163
Triandis, Henry C., 167

Underhill, Evelyn, 7, 27, 43, 101-2, 181
Ungnad, Arthur, 74, 123, 181

Vermes, Geza, 181
Versnel, Hendrik S., 165
Volz, Paul, 181
Vos, Cas J. A., 167

Wagenaar, Jan A., 168
Wagner, Roy, 165-66
Watts, James W., 168
Wellhausen, Julius, 43, 181
Wells, Jo Bailey, 166
Wells, Samuel, 172
Werline, Rodney A., 171
Westermann, Claus, 168
Wetter, Gilles P., 14, 24, 181
Weule, Karl, 10, 181
Widengren, Geo, x, 7, 11, 14, 18, 30, 37, 66, 92, 148, 164-66, 168-72, 179, 182
Will, Robert, 7, 27, 182
Witzel, Maurus, 80, 120, 182
Wright, David P., 166, 172
Wyatt, Nicolas, 170

Zeusse, Evan M., 168
Zevit, Ziony, 164
Zimmern, Heinrich, 120, 123, 182

www.ingramcontent.com/pod-product-compliance
Lightning Source LLC
Chambersburg PA
CBHW031819220426
43662CB00007B/717